KENTUCKY
Horse Tales

KENTUCKY
Horse Tales

ERCEL ELLIS JR.

Foreword by Robert W. Copelan, DVM
Introduction by Michael Blowen, Old Friends

THE
History
PRESS

Published by The History Press
Charleston, SC
www.historypress.com

First published 2019

Manufactured in the United States

ISBN 9781467141475

Library of Congress Control Number: 2019936993

Notice: The information in this book is true and complete to the best of our knowledge. It is offered without guarantee on the part of the author or The History Press. The author and The History Press disclaim all liability in connection with the use of this book.

Contents

Contents

Contents

Foreword

Red Wingfield was an old horse trainer back when I was a race track veterinarian. His foreman, Red Bolus, often spoke of horses long forgotten, and would say, "There ain't many of us old boys left." That expression stuck with me, and as the years passed, it meant more and more. Ercel Ellis has written a book, now that he's one of the "old boys," titled *Kentucky Horse Tales*. It includes many tales of personal experience, horses he knew and some he grew up with, Mata Hari, Spy Song and Man o' War. These are fascinating stories, and I bet a lot of us "old boys" still remember where they were and what they were doing on November 1, 1947, when they heard that Man o' War had died.

—Robert W. Copelan, DVM

Acknowledgements

Never in this world did I imagine that someday I would try to write a book, but after some twenty years of talking about horses on *Horse Tales*, the two-hour radio show that I do every Saturday morning, friends began to ask if I would. Jackie, my wife of many years, began to, dare I say, nag me about it until out of self-defense I told her I would give it a shot. Little did she know what she was getting into. Thank you, Jackie. Special thanks to my friend and confidant Dr. Bob Copelan for his advice and encouragement and friend Murray D. West, MD, who patiently helped with proofreading. I am going to tell you up front that I did precious little research but depended on a somewhat faulty memory and the small library that I have put together over the years. I write about horses that I grew up with, many you may have never heard of, but I remember them because they were part of my past, which is approaching nine decades. I wanted to write about past champions that had been largely forgotten, horses such as Dark Mirage, El Chico, Blue Peter, By Jimminy, champions all that should be remembered. I have barely scratched the surface there. Thanks also to the lovely people at the Keeneland Library and to the many friends acquired through the years, especially those who have stuck with me as sponsors of the radio show. You know who you are, and I am afraid of leaving someone out if I began a list. Finally, thanks to my dad for introducing me to Man o' War and teaching me to love the Thoroughbred, and to my mother for reading to me as a child and for hauling my little behind to the public library in Lexington as soon as

I was old enough to have a library card. Without her, I might never have read the *Blood-Horse* or discovered the writings of John Taintor Foote, Joe Palmer, Joe Estes, Abe Hewitt, Kent Hollingsworth, Ed Bowen or the many others who have written about the Thoroughbred with authority and grace. I must admit that writing this brought back pleasant memories of the many horses that have touched my life or fired my imagination through the years. I hope you enjoy reading about them.

Introduction

By Michael Blowen, Old Friends Inc.

The voice seems to come up through the same limestone and blue grass that made Man o' War the greatest horse of all time. It's a voice that has been invited into homes throughout Kentucky for many decades—whether it was relaying the day's race results long before the internet or telling stories on his long-running radio show, *Horse Tales*. All of us who love racing owe an enormous debt of gratitude to my friend, Ercel Ellis.

Just as we might have thought that Ercel has given us enough, he gives us more. You are very fortunate to be holding this remarkable memoir in your hands. And, as you might have predicted, the stories in this book are more about the sport than Ercel. I'm sure that's the way he wants it.

Personally, Ercel was the first person of influence in racing to help publicize aftercare when it was in its infancy. When others scoffed and ridiculed the idea, he embraced it. At the core, he realized that what was good for the athletes was good for the sport.

Whether recounting the ups and downs of his career as a trainer or as a writer and editor for various publications such as the *Daily Racing Form* and the *Blood-Horse*, Ercel never resorts to self-aggrandizement because it's rarely about him—it's about the horses and personalities. And every Thoroughbred or human athlete fortunate enough to fall under Ercel's literary spell owes him a deep debt of gratitude. We are all fortunate that Ercel spent many hours recalling stories that are unique to him. For without him, the horse tales would've disappeared, and that would be a tremendous loss to the Sport of Kings and serfs. We can never repay that debt, but we can indulge in the great pleasure of reading the unmistakable voice that has done for racing as much as his idol, Joe Palmer. I can't wait to read the sequel.

My Dad and Man o' War

My dad, Ercel Ellis Sr., was born in 1892 in Peaks Mill, Kentucky, which is in Franklin County, also home to Frankfort, the state capital. He used to tease his mother, who lived with us the last few years of her life, that he came out of Peaks Mill on a grapevine. "First time I saw a train, over in Frankfort, it scared me so bad I ran up under the station platform and they had to feed me on a plank for three days." Dad never let the truth stand in the way of a good story, a character flaw passed on to me.

At some stage in his life, his family moved to Lexington, where his father had obtained a job as county jailer. He attended the old Morton High School in Lexington, which was on the southeast corner of what is now Martin Luther King Boulevard and Short Street. He was an all-state fullback on a team that lost but one game, that to the state university team, 16–0. A few years later, in 1916, the state university team evolved into what is now the University of Kentucky Wildcats. Don't know if they called themselves the Wildcats when they played Morton High. Dad always described them as "those dirty bastards."

Dad's first job with horses was with August Belmont's Nursery Stud, which was a couple of miles north of Lexington on the Georgetown Pike. On March 29, 1917, he went to work and put the first halter on a chestnut colt by Fair Play out of Mahubah, by Rock Sand, that was later named Man o' War. I was to grow up with tales of Man o' War, some of which may have even been true. But they were all fun and let me admit up front that I was in awe of the horse—to me, he is still the greatest ever to step on a racetrack.

ad went into the army a few months after his first meeting with Man o'
r. Because he was a horseman, he was assigned to the cavalry, then later
ansferred to the field artillery. They still used horses in the field artillery.
Dad then shipped from here to France. He talked about his trip over. "For
the first half of the trip I was so seasick I thought I was going to die. For
the second half, I was afraid I wasn't." He arrived in France just in time
for the Armistice, turned around and came home, bringing his saddle and
his helmet. That helmet was useless. Later on, I put a hole in it with a 22
short that you could put your thumb through. The saddle was the most
uncomfortable I ever sat in. I would've deserted.

In 1929, Dad went to work at Dixiana as assistant manager for Charles T.
Fisher. Dixiana was as it is today located some six miles north of Lexington
on Russell Cave Road. In fact, the main farm entrance is just across the
road from the Russell Cave. Mr. Fisher, a lovely man, had purchased
Dixiana from the estate of James Cox Brady. He, with his brothers, had
started in business as blacksmiths specializing in making buggies. This
soon evolved into making bodies for Chevrolets, Pontiacs, Oldsmobiles,
Buicks and Cadillacs. Body by Fisher. His motive for buying Dixiana was
that his daughter, Mary V., loved horses and was active with Saddlebreds.
So Dixiana under Mr. Fisher started out breeding Saddlebreds and
Thoroughbreds and became highly successful in both fields. Dad was
named manager several years later, and I was to grow up on the farm,
which was just a short bike ride from Faraway Farm, home of Man o' War.
Dad was to stay at Dixiana until his death in 1964.

MAN O' WAR

I was born on May 30, 1931, and probably six years old when Dad first took
me to see Man o' War. "Take a good look at this horse, boy, you'll never see
another one like him." That was over eighty years ago. And he was right.

August Belmont II, breeder of Man o' War, volunteered his services when
World War I broke out and received a commission at the age of sixty-five. It
had been his custom to race his homebreds, but because of military activities,
he decided to sell all but six of the twenty-nine that comprised the yearling
crop of 1918. He retained five fillies and one colt. The fillies were retained
as future broodmares, and Belmont obviously knew what he was doing. All
five became distinguished producers. The colt was Man o' War.

Ercel F. Ellis Sr., longtime manager of Dixiana Farm. Dad put the first halter on Man o' War when he was foaled on March 29, 1917. *Author's collection.*

Joe Estes, editor of the *Blood-Horse* magazine, years later was to write of Man o' War that "almost from the beginning he was to touch the imagination of men." Belmont must've seen something in him as well. Man o' War was not prepped for the sale, and this turned out to be a blessing. It was the custom to fatten yearlings up for sales as a means of hiding flaws. On July 24, 1918, Belmont wrote to Elizabeth Kane, who had taken over as farm manager on the death of her husband, Edward, that he had decided to add Man o' War to the sale. The sale was to be held at Saratoga and was scheduled for August 17. That left precious little time for sale prep. Louis Feustal had been to the farm to inspect the yearlings for Riddle, which were first offered for sale privately and then as a package group, and he remembered Man o' War as a "tall gangly colt." But he liked him. So, Man o' War went through the ring, and Riddle bought him for $5,000, which seems ridiculously low but was the third-best price of the sale. The likely under bidder was R.L. Gerry, who was looking for a hunter.

Man o' War, when his racing career ended, arrived in Kentucky on January 27, 1921, spending the night at the old Kentucky Association Track in Lexington. The next day he came out to canter before a crowd of admirers then was taken to Hinata Farm where he was to stand his first and also a good portion of his second season at stud. Hinata Farm, located on the southeast corner of Russell Cave and Iron Works Pike, was under lease to Elizabeth Dangerfield. Miss Dangerfield's father had managed James R. Keene's Castleton Farm. She was actively supervising property purchased by Riddle and Walter Jeffords, who was married to Mrs. Riddle's niece, that had been purchased from the back of Mount Brilliant Farm on the Huffman Mill Pike and named Faraway Farm by the partners.

Man o' War was placed under the care of groom John Buckner, who was employed by Miss Dangerfield and who had previously taken care of the great stallions at Castleton. The story goes that shortly after Man o' War was turned out at Hinata Miss Dangerfield looked out her office window and there he was at a dead run in his paddock. Calling out the door to Buckner she said, "John catch that horse before he kills himself." "Miss Josephine," he hollered back, "if all them good horses in New York couldn't ketch him, how you 'spect me to?" He was to stay with Man o' War until Miss Dangerfield retired because of poor health in 1930. That's when Will Harbut took over Buckner's duties as Man o' War's groom.

Traffic wasn't bad on the Russell Cave Pike back then so I could ride my bike over to Faraway Farm in about fifteen or twenty minutes to see Man o' War. Dad told me to stay out of the way, don't wear out your welcome and call Will Harbut Mr. Harbut. Mr. Harbut was to stay with Man o' War for seventeen years.

Man o' War's grandsire, Hastings, had been vicious. His sire, Fair Play, was a hellion. Man o' War had beautiful manners. Mr. Harbut would, many

Man o' War and longtime groom Will Harbut. Note that the shank is merely snapped in the halter ring. *Bert Clark Tayer, photographer.*

times, just snap the shank to the ring of the halter to turn him out. Man o' War would stand still until Mr. Harbut stepped back, and then he would explode into a dead run. The power would take your breath away—remember, the horse was twenty years old when I first saw him.

Visits were mostly during summer vacations, and I can't ever remember being there without tourists about. Mr. Harbut was a showman. Writers referred to his "rich dialect" but I suspect that it was a bit richer when entertaining visitors. He also had a sense of humor. Back in the '30s, headlines around the nation trumpeted the arrival of the Dionne Quintuplets in Canada, five little girls. The story goes that the parents visited Man o' War and the father told Mr. Harbut, "I can't wait to see Man o' War," to which the reply was, "He's sure been looking forward to seeing you, too."

A description of Man o' War is difficult. He just didn't look like other Thoroughbreds. People who didn't know which end of the horse the tail was on would see a picture and say, "That's Man o' War!" Joe H. Palmer, considered in this corner to be the greatest journalist ever to write about horses, described him as "being as near to a living flame as horses ever get, and horses get closer to this than anything else."

Palmer also wrote of watching Man o' War free in his paddock: "All horses, particularly all stallions, like to run, exultant in their strength and power. Most of them run within themselves, as children run at play. But Man o' War, loose in his paddock at Faraway, dug in as if the Prince of all the fallen angels were at his throat latch and great chunks of sod sailed up behind the lash of his power. Watching, you felt that there had never been, nor ever could be again, a horse like this." Amen!

Years after Man o' War's retirement, his trainer Louis Feustal was asked if he had ever "given him something to make him run." Testing for drugs was lax at that time. Feustal replied that "all that horse ever wanted to do was run, and I would have been afraid to give him anything." He is reported to also have said that Man o' War was no trouble to handle. On one occasion, though, Man o' War did toss his exercise rider and wander about the track at Saratoga for some twenty minutes before being caught. The only time he was unruly was at the break of his races; occasionally, he caused a delay. At that time, there were no starting gates and horses broke from behind a webbing. "He just wanted to go," Feustal allowed.

There was absolutely no chance of hiding Man o' War before he got to the races. Early on, a clocker watched him breeze and walked down to ask the groom, "Who's the big chestnut colt by?" The groom's reply was "by hisself, mostly." I thought it was interesting that one of the five first crop stakes winners sired by Man o' War was named By Hisself.

Man o' War did develop one bad habit as a stallion. He became unruly when taken out of his stall to cover a mare, rearing up and flaying with his fore legs. Harrie Scott, who had taken over the management of Faraway Farm upon the departure of Elizabeth Dangerfield in 1930, claimed that Man o' War was the smartest horse he had ever been around. He told Riddle that he could cure that but that there was a risk involved. Given the green light, when Man o' War went up, Scott pulled him over backward. Observers said the horse landed with a thud that shook the barn, got up, shook himself and thereafter walked on all four feet.

MAN O' WAR AT STUD

Man o' War entered stud for a fee of $2,500, no return. No return meant that if your mare didn't get in foal, tough luck. After his first crop hit the tracks in 1924, it went up to $5,000, but few seasons were offered to outside breeders. His first crop consisted of but thirteen foals, seven colts and six fillies. One of the fillies was never named, so I assume she died, but five of the twelve named foals became stakes winners.

The first Man o' War foal to start was the filly Lightship, bred by Jeffords. She never won a race but later produced two stakes winners. The first to win was American Flag, bred by Riddle. The next year American Flag was undefeated in four starts to rank at the top of his class after taking the classic Belmont Stakes, the Withers and the Dwyer. Two fillies from the first crop also won classic races. Jeffords's Florence Nightingale won the Coaching Club American Oaks and Riddles' Maid at Arms the Alabama. That was the beginning of a great career at stud, a career that could've been greater had he been provided better quality mares.

Riddle, it seems, reached the conclusion that you could breed anything to Man o' War and he would sire you a runner. For instance, what is generally considered to be his greatest runner, Triple Crown winner War Admiral, was out of the tiny mare Brush Up, by Sweep. She stood 14.3 hands and couldn't outrun a fat man. Still, at career's end, he had sired 17 percent stakes winners. Among those foals was champion Crusader, considered by many to be the best son of Man o' War, over War Admiral. These days, breeders would flock to any stallion that was siring 17 percent stakes winners from foals.

War Admiral, the 1937 Triple Crown winner, looked about as much like his sire as I do Robert Redford. He was registered as brown—these days, it would have been dark bay or brown—and was not a big horse. His dam was by Sweep, who had a tendency to sire small individuals. Riddle didn't like War Admiral and offered to sell him as a yearling to Jeffords. Jeffords seriously considered taking Riddle up on his offer but decided not to. Riddle could be a bit cantankerous at times, and Jeffords was afraid that if the colt turned out to be a runner it might cause problems in the family. I wonder if there were regrets later on.

A son of Man o' War won the Kentucky Derby in 1929. The gelding, Clyde Van Dusen, named after his trainer, led all the way in the mud after breaking from post position 20 in the field of 21. Van Dusen later moved to California and used the gelding as a lead pony.

Fair Play, sire of Man o' War. That's Al Kane, son of farm manager Mrs. Edward Kane, on the shank. *L.S. Sutcliffe, photographer.*

All told, Man o' War sired sixty-four stakes winners. Man o' War topped the sire list in 1926 and ranked among the leaders nine times and among the leading broodmare sires twenty-two times. His sire line lives on today, largely through Tiznow and his sons.

MAN O' WAR'S FUNERAL

In May 1947 my visits, save one, ended. Faraway was closed to visitors because Man o' War was not doing well. Man o' War died a little after noon on November 1 that year. Mr. Harbut had preceded him, passing away following a stroke on October 3. My last visit was to Man o' War's funeral at Faraway with my father. It was a typical early November day, chilly but pleasant. We had to walk a couple of hundred yards past Domino's grave and where Herbert Hazelton's larger-than-life statue of the horse was to be placed. Some people, Harrie Scott included, did not care for the statue. I like the fact that it is larger than life. So was Man o' War.

There was a nice crowd. I have seen estimates of between one and two thousand. Dad and I stayed on the fringe, away from the open casket. Neither of us wanted to remember him that way. The speakers were an illustrious group. First was Ira Drymon, who operated Gallagher Farm, where Polynesian, sire of Native Dancer, was later to stand at stud. Automobile dealer Charles Sturgill followed, extolling how Man o' War had meant so much to the economy of Lexington. There was Leslie Combs II, master of Spendthrift Farm; A.B. "Bull" Hancock Jr. of Claiborne Farm; Neville Dunn of the weekly trade magazine *Thoroughbred Record*; Joe Estes, editor of another weekly trade magazine, the *Blood-Horse*; then Faraway Farm manager Patrick O'Neill; Keeneland president Louis Lee Haggin; and Dr. William McGee, who had given Man o' War a sedative to spare him pain as he fought to rise as death approached. Palmer wrote of those final moments, "A lesser horse might have been, in mercy, destroyed, but Man o' War must finish out the course. He would have wanted it that way."

Mr. Drymon concluded the eulogy by saying, "Truly he was a memorable horse. Almost from the beginning he touched the imagination of men, and they all saw different things in him. But one thing they will all remember. That he brought an exultation into their hearts." Dad and I left shortly after that, before they lowered the casket. I had glanced over at Dad during the ceremony, and he had tears in his eyes. The only other time I ever saw him tear up was when I left for the service, and those were likely tears of relief.

Questions of Man o' War's lone defeat, in the Sanford Stakes at Saratoga, have endured much speculation through the years. Mr. Harbut blamed it on the jockey, John Loftus, and he may have been partially right. Rumors that he was facing the wrong way at the break are not accurate. The rider of the winner that day, Willie Knapp, told it this way years later, and he was in a position to know:

> *When the field bounced away it was Golden Broom settin' the pace, with Upset on the outside just a neck away. Man o' War didn't make his bid until we hit the turn, and then he churned up along the rail till his head bobbed in the corner of my eye. There he was, tossin' those 28-foot strides of his an' tryin' to squeeze through on the inside of Golden Broom and Upset. If I had given so much of an inch the race would've been over, but jockeys don't ride that way. I could of breezed past Golden Broom anytime I took my feet off the dashboard, but that would also have let Man o' War out of his mousetrap and he would have whooshed past us in half a dozen strides. When Johnny Loftus saw we weren't goin' to open up there was*

only one thing left for him to do. He pulled up sharply and ducked to the outside. That's what I've been waiting for. That same moment I gunned Upset with my bat and galloped to the lead in a couple of jumps. Man o' War then had to come around the two of us and it cost him all of two lengths. From there to the finish he was charging again like a jet plane but Upset had just enough left to push his head down in front.

Knapp went on to say that "it was the biggest thrill of my life, but looking back on it now there's sure one horse that should've retired unbeaten. If I moved over just an eyelash that day at Saratoga he would beat me from here to jalopy. Sometimes I'm sorry I didn't do it."

"Joe" Estes, turf writer, wrote the following:

Big Red

The days are long at Belmont,
Speed they never learn.
And it's many a day since Man o' War
Has looped the upper turn.

The guineas stopped their rubbing,
The rider dropped his tack
When the word went round that Man o' War
Was coming on the track.

The crowd was hoarse with cheering
At ancient Pimlico
The day he won the Preakness—
But that was long ago.

The dust is deep at Windsor,
The good old days are done,
And many a horse is forgotten,
But they still remember one.

For he was a fiery phantom
To that multitudinous throng—
Would you wait for another one like him?
Be patient: years are long.

My Dad and Man o' War

For here was a horse among horses,
Cast in a Titan's mold,
And the slant October sunlight
Gilded the living gold.

He was marked with the gods' own giving
And winged in every part;
The look of eagles was in his eye
And Hastings' wrath in his heart.

Young Equipoise had power
To rouse the crowded stand,
And there was magic in the name
Of Greentree's Twenty Grand,

And Sarazan has sprinted,
And Gallant Fox has stayed,
And Discovery has glittered
In the wake of Cavalcade…

We watch the heroes parading,
We wait, and our eyes are dim,
But we never discover another
Like him.

*   *   *

A foal is born at midnight
And in the frosty morn
The horseman eyes him fondly,
And a secret hope is born,
But breathe it not, nor whisper,
For fear of a neighbor's scorn:
He's a chestnut colt, and he's got a star—
He may be another Man o' War.

Nay, say it aloud—be shameless:
Dream and hope and yearn,
For there's never a man among you
But waits for his return.

2

C. T. Fisher and the History of Dixiana

HISTORY OF DIXIANA

Major Barak G. Thomas purchased Hamilton Stud in 1877 and renamed it Dixiana after his favorite mare, Dixie. He was the breeder of Himyar, sire of both Domino and Plaudit, sire lines that survive today. Major Thomas, a native of Lexington and a Confederate veteran, sold Dixiana in 1892 to Jacob S. Coxey of Massillon, Ohio, and moved much of his stock to nearby Hira Villa Farm. Hira was the dam of Himyar, and it is believed that it was at Hira Villa that Domino was foaled. Both were sections of what is now Mt. Brilliant Farm.

Coxey was devoted to Standardbreds, and he did not stay long, selling Dixiana to Thomas J. Carson from Mississippi, like Major Thomas a Confederate veteran. Carson also purchased a dozen mares and the young stallion prospect Ben Strome, a son of Ben d'Or, from Major Thomas, and therein lies a story.

Ben Strome was an unlikely sire prospect. He had been just a so-so runner, and his female family was not the strongest in the books. He got off to a slow start at stud when his first foals reached racing age. Thomas also raised fighting chickens, and they were not doing well either. This prompted a farmhand to remark to Carson that "it's too bad them Ben Stromes can't run like them chickens!"

Ben Strome, however, beat the odds and topped the sire list in 1903. Don't know about the chickens. He was the sire of one of the all-time great sprinters, Roseben, bred by Mrs. Carson. Roseben was a great favorite with fans and was dubbed the "Big Train." He was huge, standing 17.3 hands. He also was a great weight carrier, winning on four occasions under 147 pounds and running second under 150. He set the world record for seven furlongs of 1:22 flat at Belmont in 1906, and the record remained the fastest at the distance at Belmont until 1957, when it was broken by Bold Ruler. I would be suspect of anyone who did not include Roseben among the ten best sprinters of the twentieth century. Now, I have a confession to make.

Several years ago, an acquaintance opened a bar in Lexington, and on the wall he wanted lists, by categories, of the best horses of the twentieth century. I duly submitted lists, but by an act of pure stupidity, I wrote in the name of Old Rosebud instead of Roseben. I was ashamed to go into that bar after that! Now, Old Rosebud was a terrific racehorse—he won forty races during his career, among them the 1914 Kentucky Derby—but Roseben could have pulled a wagon and beat him sprinting. The only thing they had in common was that they were both geldings.

Once Man o' War completed his three-year-old season, his owner, Samuel D. Riddle, asked Walter Vosburgh, handicapper for the Jockey Club at the time, what weight he would put on Man o' War if he raced at four. The reply was, "If he wins his first start, the highest ever carried by a Thoroughbred." I wonder if Riddle had Roseben in mind when he retired Man o' War to stud.

In 1909, Dixiana farm was once again under new ownership. It was reported that Carson traded it to Ben Ali Haggin and it became part of Haggin's Elmendorf Farm. For the next seventeen years, it was used primarily for crops and tobacco. In 1925, James Cox Brady from New York bought the property from Haggin and spent a substantial amount of money to renovate the farm, only to pass away three years later. In 1928, Mr. Fisher purchased the farm.

I don't know who was advising Mr. Fisher at the time he purchased Dixiana. The first manager at Dixiana under Mr. Fisher was Ross Long, and it was likely he. My Dad thought the world of him. Anyway, several purchases were made that were to pay big dividends for several decades. First of all, he acquired the stallion High Time. Then he obtained two broodmares, Miss Jemima, by Black Toney, and War Woman, by Man o' War, and the half-brothers Sweep All and Peter Hastings. Sweep All, a son of Sweep, and Peter Hastings, by Peter Pan, were both out of Nettie Hastings by Hastings. He obtained several other broodmares of note, but it was High Time, through his daughters, Miss Jemima and her daughters, War Woman, Sweep All and

Peter Hastings that were to establish Dixiana as one of the most successful breeding farms in the nation, with a broodmare band that never exceeded fifteen or sixteen mares.

HIGH TIME

High Time was a foal of 1916, and he was intensely inbred to Domino. His sire was Ultimus by Commando, a son of Domino, and his dam was a daughter of Domino. High Time's dam was Noonday by Domino. Thus three of the seven males in the first three generations of High Time's pedigree were by Domino. He was bred by the Wickcliff Stud of Price McKinney and James Corrigan, but the mating was reportedly arranged by Elizabeth Dangerfield.

Much of the tale of High Time was gleaned through the writings of Abraham Hewitt, a friend of Colonel Phil T. Chinn. High Time raced for the partnership of Sam Ross and Admiral Carey Grayson, of Washington, D.C., and was trained as a three-year-old by Colonel Chinn, one of the most colorful characters in racing and breeding. Colonel Chinn said that High Time could outwork any horse that ever drew breath in the morning, but he was the only horse he'd ever seen that could "come into the home stretch on top by 15 and get beat by 80." That's a bit of an exaggeration, but the Colonel was prone to that.

High Time won one race as a two-year-old, the Hudson Stakes at five furlongs, and the Colonel had taken over his training at three. He worked in sensational fashion for the Colonel, who was sure that he was going to make a killing with the bookmakers, so he bet heavily in his first start at three. High Time opened a big lead, then stopped to a walk. When his owners came back to the barn after the race, the Colonel told them, "If you get that horse out of my barn by sundown, there will be no training bill—otherwise the charges will be doubled."

High Time was retired to stud in Virginia, but he was later moved back to Kentucky. Three years later, Colonel Chinn and High Time's paths crossed again. A good friend of the Colonel's, Hiram Steele, told him that Dr. Marius Johnston had a pair of yearlings that he wanted him to look at. Even though he thought Steele to be a great judge of yearlings, the Colonel begged off. He knew that although Dr. Johnston had a great deal of money, he would be unlikely to invest much in stud fees. According to the Colonel, Dr. Johnston

High Time, champion sire in 1928 and also a champion sire of two-year-olds. *L.S. Sutcliffe, photographer.*

invested in stocks and bonds and was so nervous that "every time the stock market went down two points, they had to take him to the hospital."

But Steele kept after him and talked him into going to take a look. "My Lord," the Colonel said, "they were standouts!" So the Colonel, accompanied by Steele, went to the house to ask Dr. Johnston what he wanted for the pair. The answer was $2,500, and the Colonel replied, "They are mine." So, they sat down to have a couple of toddies to cement the deal, and finally, the Colonel asked how the colts were bred. The reply was, "They are both by High Time." "Doctor," said the Colonel, "if I had known that, I would've paid you $2,500 not to come here, but my word is my bond so I will keep them." One of the colts was the great gelding Sarazan, and the other was Time Exposure, a stakes winner of twenty-two races.

It didn't take Colonel Chinn long to figure out that both Sarazan and Time Exposure were highly talented, so much so that he thought it would be a good idea to buy High Time. The asking price was $50,000, and the Colonel was a bit low on capital. He had a good friend, W.T. "Fatty" Anderson, who was on the West Coast at the time. Anderson was a professional horseman and gambler, and like the Colonel, he spent much of his life either flush with money or broke. The Colonel sent a wire to

Anderson, asking, "Could you spare $25,000 at this time?" figuring he could come up with the balance. A few days later, he got his answer; "Any man that needs $25,000 can use $50,000." Fatty.

In 1929, High Time topped the North American Sire List, and he was a sensational sire of two-year-olds. In seventeen years at stud, he sired 289 named foals, and 57 percent of them won as two-year-olds. Unheard of! In 1929, the Colonel had fallen on hard times again, and Mr. Fisher bought High Time from him at his dispersal sale.

That was the last time High Time was to change hands. The exact numbers have long ago slipped my mind, but I recall Dad saying that at one meeting at Churchill Downs they had carded something like twenty races for two-year-olds and Dixiana won fifteen of them with High Times. The first stakes winners bred by Mr. Fisher were Esseff and In High, both by High Time, and his daughters were instrumental in the success of Dixiana. High Time, in addition to leading the General Sire List in 1929, ranked among the top ten on five other occasions, led the two-year-old sire list three times and the broodmare sire list twice. He died at Dixiana in 1937.

Incidentally, Colonel Chinn's friend Hiram Steele married the Colonel's daughter, and their son, Hal, became a successful trainer. He nearly won the 1967 Kentucky Derby with a colt named Barb's Delight, a front-running second to Proud Clarion. When I applied for my trainer's license, many moons ago, it was required that an active trainer with a good reputation endorse the applicant, and Hal was kind enough to do so for me.

ESSEFF AND IN HIGH

The first two stakes winners bred by Mr. Fisher were Esseff and In High, both foals of 1930 and both by High Time. In High won the Bashford Manor Stakes as a two-year-old and six other races and was out of a daughter of Uncle named Indiscretion. Indiscretion produced two more stakes winners for Dixiana: Leading Article and Foolish Moment. Leading Article was a colt by Supremus. He won thirty-five races, among them the Dixie Handicap and three other stakes. Foolish Moment, by High Time, won the Clipsetta Stakes and ran second in the Bashford Manor as a two-year-old and later produced Sound Barrier, the only stakes winner sired by the shy breeder Star Reward. Sound Barrier won thirty-eight races, including the Troy Stakes. I remember Foolish Moment, but the one I remember most was Esseff.

Esseff was a beautiful mare, a chestnut like most of High Time's offspring, athletic, very feminine, good size. Her first four foals all won. The first, a colt by Sweep All named All Time High, won seven times and placed in stakes. The third was Adda Pearl, by War Admiral, and she produced a good stakes winner, Golden Admiral. Her last foal was Wee One, another daughter of Sweep All; Wee One produced Lyle's First, who ran second in the Arkansas Derby. In 1942 or 1943, Esseff was sent to Virginia to be bred and came back infected and never produced another foal. I remember Dad saying that would be the last time he would ever send a mare out of state to be bred. The farm did, of course, but he would fuss about it.

Esseff, incidentally, was a half sister to Chasar, a son of Crusader and a very high-class stakes winner for Dixiana; to the dam of Snark, a son of Boojum and winner of the Suburban, Metropolitan and a bunch of other stakes; to Edelweiss, winner of the C.C.A. Oaks; and to Past Eight, dam of Times Tested and Lady Be Good, both by the King Ranch stallion Better Self. Time Tested went to stud at Carter Thornton's Threave Main Stud in Bourbon County and did quite well.

I was very fond of Carter. At one time we shared a barn at the Thoroughbred Training Center, and he was fun to be around. Tough and gruff with a heart of gold. I remember he told me that he was keeping a retired lead pony at Threave Main for a trainer friend, I think it was Syl Vietch. I asked him if he was charging board, and he said to me, "No. Well, he's paying expenses." A couple of weeks went by, and I teased him about charging board on a pony and I bet the pony had checked out years ago. The very next morning, the first thing he said when I got to the barn was "Damn you, Ellis, I went home yesterday and found that pony dead in the paddock." Knowing Carter, he may have very well been pulling my leg. Additionally, Carter may have the record for selling Kentucky Derby winners at auction, having sold Gallahadian, Hoop Jr. and Canonero.

SWEEP ALL AND PETER HASTINGS

Half-brothers Sweep All and Peter Hastings were purchased privately by Mr. Fisher. Sweep All was a foal of 1928 by Sweep out of Nettie Hastings, by Hastings, and Peter Hastings, by Peter Pan out of Nettie Hastings, was a foal of 1925. Sweep All was gorgeous. Like many of the progeny of Sweep,

Sweep All in training at the Kentucky Association track, April 16, 1931. Four weeks later, he ran second to Twenty Grand in the Kentucky Derby. *H.C. Ashley, photographer.*

he was on the small side but beautifully balanced. He was what was then called a "blood bay," with black points, black mane and tail and black on all four legs with no white markings. He won the Endurance Stakes and ran second in the Walden as a two-year-old before running a dead game second to Greentree Stable's Twenty Grand, a son of St. Germans, in the 1931 Kentucky Derby. Sweep All was virtually a private stud at Dixiana, never receiving many mares from outside breeders. But he sired a lot of runners for Dixiana and was an excellent broodmare sire.

Sweep All's best were probably Sirocco, Four Winds and Bayview. Sirocco won the 1940 Arlington Classic, beating Bimelech. George Woolf rode him that day, and he won by seven. Four Winds resembled her sire, and she won three major stakes in Chicago: the Arlington Lassie, the Princess Doreen and the Arlington Matron. For years, they featured a stakes race named after her at Arlington Park. She was a bleeder and lightly raced, winning six of her nine career starts. Bayview won the 1941 Santa Anita Handicap, beating Mioland and Bolingbroke. Harold Jordan, a great guy, was assistant manager at Dixiana at the time, and he was listening to a broadcast of the race while driving on Russell Cave Road and got so excited he ran off the road. Had to send a pair of mules to pull him out of the ditch, as they didn't have a tractor at Dixiana at that time. Working the one-mile track, in addition to all the mowing, was done with a pair of mules, Pearl and Maude.

Peter Hastings was unraced, but he sired Mata Hari, the best runner ever bred at Dixiana by Mr. Fisher. Mata Hari was a daughter of War Woman, by Man o' War. Mata Hari was the champion two-year-old filly and leading money-winning filly of 1933 and later the dam of the very successful sire Spy Song, by Balladier. For sheer, blinding speed, I have seen few that were Spy Song's equal. Mata Hari topped the Experimental Free Handicap in 1933 with an assignment of 122 pounds, 4 more than Far Star, her stablemate at Dixiana. Add the 5 pounds sex allowance, and Mata Hari was ranked superior to the colts. The top-weighted colt was First Minstrel, a son of Royal Minstrel with an assignment of 126 pounds. Cavalcade, the next year's Kentucky Derby winner, was assigned 125.

3

Dixiana Broodmares

MISS JEMIMA

One of the first acquisitions to the Dixiana broodmare band by Mr. Fisher was Miss Jemima. She was a foal of 1917, thus from the same crop as Man o' War. She even ran against him in the Futurity and was generally conceded to be the best two-year-old filly of the year in a year of talented fillies, such as Cleopatra, Constancy and Bonnie Mary, who were from the same crop. During her two-year-old year, Miss Jemima put together a string of seven wins, four of them in stakes, and she whipped colts in the Flash Stakes carrying 129 pounds. Quite a feat—she wasn't as big as a minute.

Miss Jemima was bred by Colonel E.R. Bradley and was by the Idle Hour stallion Black Toney out of Vaila, a daughter of the Irish stallion Fariman. Vaila was imported by Bradley. Why he sold Miss Jemima I don't know; he usually raced and was not in the habit of selling. Maybe it was because she was small. He used to test his two-year-olds over the track on his farm, so perhaps he didn't like what he saw. At any rate, Miss Jemima raced for C.E. Rowe, and I assume that Mr. Fisher acquired her from Rowe. Great move. She produced eleven foals for Dixiana. Six earned blacktype, and more importantly, her daughters and granddaughters produced a long string of stakes winners.

Miss Jemima's pedigree was all Bradley. He owned her sire and her dam. She was a full sister to Broadway Jones, winner of the then important Latonia

Derby and other stakes, and also a full sister to the unraced Bridal Colors, dam of Relic, winner of the 1947 Hopeful Stakes and later a very successful sire in France. She was a half sister to Pimlico Futurity winner Blossom Time, by the Idle Hour stallion North Star III, and the dam of champion Blue Larkspur by Black Servant. Blue Larkspur was a colt considered by many, including yours truly, to be the best that Bradley ever bred. I guess most give the nod to Bimelech a decade later, but I was never too high on Bimelech. I thought him overrated. I have a picture of Dixiana's Sirocco beating him by seven lengths in the Arlington Classic. Blue Larkspur won the Belmont Stakes in 1929, the Classic in Chicago, Withers Stakes, Arlington Cup and the Stars and Stripes after winning the Saratoga Special and the Juvenile Stakes at two. He was the favorite for the Kentucky Derby, but the track came up heavy and the win went to the Man o' War gelding Clyde Van Dusen. Blue Larkspur was a very successful sire and an even better broodmare sire.

The best of the eleven foals out of Miss Jemima was Far Star. Far Star was one of three stakes-winning fillies foaled in 1931 at Dixiana, the others being Mata Hari and Constant Wife. That happened to be the year of my birth, so, as my dad used to say, it was definitely a filly year. Far Star beat colts and her stablemate, Mata Hari, in the Arlington Futurity and won the Debutante Stakes at Lincoln Fields at the direct expense of Constant Wife. She also was a terrific producer for Dixiana.

Miss Jemima produced her last foal in 1941. She was twenty-four and had a difficult time foaling and looked terrible, so much so that Mr. Fisher thought she should be euthanized. Dad said okay but instead moved her to a barn that was somewhat isolated and appointed me her caretaker. I was ten at the time, and it was my job to see that Miss Jemima was fed and watered and her stall cleaned. No problem. She was a sweet old mare. I learned a lot from her, but time caught up with her and she died the following summer. I suspect that Mr. Fisher knew that we were hiding her, but he never said a word. Maybe it was because I was taking care of her. I'd like to think so.

Miss Jemima's Legacy Far Star

Far Star, one of the "big three" fillies foaled at Dixiana in 1931, was by North Star III, and she was the third foal and first stakes winner out of Miss Jemima. She was a pretty filly of medium size and a chestnut, unlike her dam, a dark bay.

Far Star after defeating colts and stablemate Mata Hari in the 1933 Arlington Futurity. *Bob White, track photographer, Arlington Park.*

North Star III, by Sunstar, won the Middlepark Stakes in England and had been imported for stud duty by Bradley. I read somewhere that his get were a bit on the temperamental side, but Far Star inherited none of it. It was perhaps because of this temperament that Bradley had refrained from breeding anything from the Hastings–Fair Play line, also well known for willfulness, until War Admiral arrived on the scene to win the Triple Crown in 1937. Perhaps he had seen War Admiral win the Belmont Stakes after grabbing a quarter coming out of the gate to stand in a pool of blood in the winners' circle. He was not to race again for five months.

Far Star's big win in 1933 came in the Arlington Futurity over colts and her stablemate Mata Hari. She went to the front and never looked back, with Mata Hari finishing fourth. Mat got into an argument with the starting crew, as she was wont to do if she was crossed, said to hell with it and was beaten by about five lengths. Mr. Fisher and her trainer, Clyde Van Dusen, were watching Mat and didn't know they had won the race until Far Star came back to the winner's circle.

Far Star also won the Debutante Stakes in Chicago that summer over stablemate Constant Wife. Constant Wife was by Chicle out of Penelope, by Sweep and had won the Hialeah Juvenile Championship Stakes earlier in the year. Unlike Far Star and Mata Hari, she was a disappointment as a broodmare. Far Star made but one start as a three-year-old, finishing second to Fiji in the Kentucky Oaks after bowing a tendon and was sent home.

Far Star was to produce four stakes winners for Dixiana: Star Boarder, Star Reward, Fleeting Star and Sabean. Star Boarder, by the home stallion Sweep All, was her first foal and he was a good one. He won seventeen races, including the Washington Park and Motor City handicaps, with placings in five more stakes. Star Reward by Whirlaway's half brother Reaping Reward came next and he won seven stakes and placed in thirteen more. He beat Coaltown in the Equipoise Mile at Arlington Park and also competed in the 1947 Kentucky Derby, the first I ever attended.

The track was labeled slow that day at Churchill Downs, but the rain had stopped by post time. Jet Pilot, bred by A.B. Hancock Sr., broke from the outside 13 post position and went right to the front under Eric Guerin. The favorite, C.V. Whitney's Phalanx, broke dead last and came fast on the outside under Eddie Arcaro with Calumet's Faultless also coming with a nice run on the rail. Seventy yards from the wire, Jet Pilot was dead tired, with Guerin just waving the whip to encourage him but never using it. I guess he knew that he was giving his all. Star Reward made a big move approaching the stretch, then flattened out. Jet Pilot hung on to win by a head over Phalanx with Faultless third another head back. Exciting finish. I can picture it in my mind just as I saw it that day.

Jet Pilot raced for Maine Chance, and he was lucky to be there. The year before, Maine Chance had a three-horse entry in the Derby of Lord Boswell, Knockdown and Perfect Bahram, and they sent Jet Pilot with them from Chicago to make his first start as a two-year-old. While they were in Kentucky, there was a fire at Arlington Park, and many of the Maine Chance horses perished. If Star Reward had not been in the race, I would've rooted for Jet Pilot.

The Derby was the last race Jet Pilot won. He ran fourth in the Preakness, won by Faultless, and finished far back in the Belmont, which went to Phalanx. That was his last start, and I'll wager that his trainer, Tom Smith, didn't want to run in that one. I'll speculate that his owner, Elizabeth Graham, made that decision. Graham changed trainers about as often as I change underwear. The running joke at the time was that there was a special section in heaven for former Maine Chance trainers but nobody wanted to go because it was too crowded.

Star Reward, by Reaping Reward, was almost black and what I would describe as refined. He went to stud at Dixiana but proved to be infertile, siring but three or four foals.

The third stakes winner out of Far Star was Fleeting Star. I always loved that name. Miss Mary had a way with naming horses. He was by Count Fleet and won the Churchill Downs Handicap as a four-year-old in 1950 under Steve Brooks. He was a nice two-year-old, finishing second in the Kentucky Jockey Club Stakes at Churchill and third in Keeneland's Breeders Futurity. He went to stud at Steve Black's Silver Lake Farm near Frankfort and sired some useful runners.

Far Star's fourth stakes winner, Sabean, arrived in 1947. Sabean won fifteen times, including the Midwest and Peninsula handicaps and set a new track record at Hawthorne going six and a half furlongs in 1:16 and 1/5. Sabean was a colt by Maryland champion Challedon. Challedon is considered by many to be the best ever foaled in Maryland—although most would give that honor to Cigar. Cigar may have been foaled in Maryland, but he was raised by Ted Carr at Brookside Farm near Versailles, which, the last time I looked, is in Kentucky. Challedon was a champion at three and Horse of the Year, but his connections kept him in training when he was past his peak. He went to stud at Ira Drymon's Gallagher's Farm and did very well.

Two daughters of Far Star produced runners of note. Saran, by St. Germans, was a good race mare, winning thirteen races in tough company. She was the dam of Here's Hoping, a black filly by Eight Thirty. Here's Hoping won the Princess Pat Stakes, Tomboy Stakes, Cleopatra Handicap and Churchill Downs Handicap. She set a new track record for six and a half furlongs at Keeneland and returned the next year to break her own track record. Here's Hoping was a disappointment as a producer, although several of her daughters became stakes producers.

Eight Thirty was at stud at George D. Widener's Old Kenny Farm right next door to Dixiana, and my goodness, he was such a good-looking horse and a heck of a sire.

Saran also was the ancestress of Make Ready and Courtier, two nice horses with whom I became closely involved. Make Ready had shown promise in the winter of 1955 and 1956 at the Fair Grounds in New Orleans while I was with the Dixiana racing stable. Jack Hodgins was the trainer. I never met the famed Ben Jones, trainer for Calumet Farm. I was taking Make Ready to the track at Keeneland—he had to be led because he was a handful—and Ben Jones was coming back on his white pony leading a horse that had already completed his workout. Mr. Jones never took his eyes off Make Ready, and when he was close, said, "I don't know who he is but I'm afraid of him." That's as close as I ever got to meeting him, but later I did get to know his son Jimmy, a great trainer in his own right. Make Ready, although he did win races, never turned out to be as good as he looked.

Several years later, I had a two-year-old for sale by Great Sun, and Jimmy Jones was looking to buy for a client. So, he came out to the farm I had leased at the time. Great Sun was a son of Bold Ruler and had sired several good runners, including the fast Hawkins Special, who held the six-furlong track record at Santa Anita. I trained my horses to come when I called, and the colt came flying up the hill and screeched to a stop. He did love peppermints. Jimmy was standing behind me, and I heard him comment about it. He still didn't buy him. Great Sun, however, did not last long. He was badly foundered. Painful to watch in the breeding shed.

Courtier was from the first crop by Cortil, a stakes winner in France at stud at Spendthrift Farm. I was breaking yearlings at Dixiana, and we had two of them, Courtier and a colt named Solution. Dad gave me those two to rub, probably because he didn't like Cortil. We were loading the yearlings to go to the racing stable and he saved my two Cortils to last. They had been contending with a bunch of Spy Song yearlings; the

Spy Songs could be a handful, and my dad's patience was running out. Finally, he bellowed, "Bring those two damn Cortils down." I did, and they walked on the van like they had been doing it all their lives. I was so proud. Courtier went on to place in stakes and set a new track record at Hawthorne in Chicago. Solution won several stakes in Chicago. Dad was right about Cortil, though. Those were probably the best things he ever sired. I was rubbing Solution in the spring of 1956. His stable name was Bull. He had just returned from the track one morning, and as I was slipping his bridle off, he threw his head around and popped me a good one. I went down like I was shot and was knocked out for a couple of seconds. Muhammad Ali couldn't have done it better. One of the wise guys in the barn said it was a good thing he hit me in the head, where it couldn't do any damage.

In 1948, Far Star produced the pretty filly Astro, by Count Fleet. Astro ran second to How in the Kentucky Oaks with Sickle's Image third. No disgrace there. How, a daughter of Princequillo, won the Coaching Club American Oaks later that year, and Sickle's Image was one of the toughest fillies around in the 1950s.

MISS PRUDENCE

(Daughter of Miss Jemima)

Miss Prudence, Miss Jemima's foal of 1933, was by Victorian, a son of Whisk Broom II. She produced ten winners that won a total of eighty-one races. Among them was a nice colt named Safety First, by Isolater. Safety First won six times and ran third in the Joliet Stakes. Her most noteworthy contribution to Dixiana was her 1942 foal by Sweep All, a filly named Little Priss.

Little Priss had speed. She was about as quick out of the gate as horses could break, but she couldn't be rated. Consequently, although she won six times, she got caught a lot. This is verified by the fact that she ran second nine times and third three times. One of the all-time great horsemen, Olin Gentry, told me once that the thing he wanted to see most in a broodmare prospect was speed. "I don't care how far they carry it, but that's the first thing I look for." He would have loved Little Priss.

She also was a little light behind, meaning she could kick a chew of tobacco out of your mouth at twenty paces. Back when she was competing, the paddock at Keeneland was open to everybody, and people would crowd around the horses as they were being saddled. I lived in mortal fear that Prissy would nail someone, but she never did. What she did do was become a terrific producer for Dixiana.

Prissy produced three stakes winners, all three by the Australian champion Bernborough. Bernborough was one of my all-time favorites. I went to the movies in Lexington, and there was a short feature on him. He began his career racing at small bush tracks in Australia, but because of a dispute over his ownership, he was not allowed to compete at the major tracks. Finally, under new ownership, he moved to the big time and won fifteen in a row carrying as much as 152 pounds or more. He would loll around in the middle of the pack then cut loose a stretch run that would bring you out of your seat. He won under 151 pounds, giving the second horse 38 pounds, and became something of a rock star in Australia. I read that it was like a funeral when he broke down, with people in tears.

Louis B. Mayer bought Bernborough, and he went to stud at Spendthrift Farm, then owned by Leslie Combs II. I went to see him. Big horse, right at 17 hands, bay, high withers, tremendous shoulder. When he arrived in Kentucky, his mane and foretop were rather long, which may have been customary in Australia at the time. He did quite well at stud, though he never commanded a big stud fee. His best was champion sprinter Berseem, out of Little Priss. When B. Wayne Hughes purchased Spendthrift a few years back, he remodeled a stud barn and put up plaques with the names of champions that had been at stud there. No Bernborough. I hounded Hughes until he put up one with the Australian stud's name. I think they put up one with Shannon II's name, another Australian, at the same time.

Berseem was the first of the three Bernboroughs out of Little Priss to win stakes. He was a foal of 1950. In 1952, Larrikin arrived, and two years later came Resolved. I was there when Berseem was foaled, and five years later I watched him run at Hollywood Park. He didn't win that day, but they had to catch him, just like his mama. In a seven-furlong race, he had a three-length lead at the eighth pole after sprinting the first six furlongs in 1:08 and 2/5, but Porterhouse caught him at the wire. Porterhouse had been co-champion two-year-old with Turn-to in 1953. He was by Endeavor II, who had been imported to this country to compete in the Washington, D.C. International. Porterhouse raced for Llangollen Farm and later went to stud at the Stallion Station in Kentucky.

Dixiana trainer Jack Hodgins sold Berseem as a three-year-old to Frank Childs, who was training for Allen Hirschberg at the time. It was a package deal. Childs wanted Berseem's stablemate, Spy Defense, the next-to-last foal produced by Mata Hari, but in order to get him, he had to take Berseem. Spy Defense had run second with Berseem third to Greentree Farms' Straight Face in the 1952 Kentucky Jockey Club Stakes at Churchill. Spy Defense, by Bull Lea, did not work out for his new connections; he was mean as a snake and ended up at stud in Nebraska. But Berseem sure did. After winning five times for Dixiana, he went to the West Coast and won sixteen more races and was named champion sprinter in 1955. He went to stud at Laguna Seca Ranch and sired a nice filly named Curious Clover.

Resolved was in the Dixiana stable at Gulfstream in the winter of 1956 and 1957, and he broke his maiden there, paying forty dollars and change to win. I didn't bet on him. Probably broke at the time. The stable went to Keeneland, then to Chicago, and Hodgins sold him to W.H. Bishop. He developed into a very good grass horse, winning six grass stakes over the next couple of years. Unlike his mama, he could handle two turns, but he still liked to go to the front.

I suspect that the reason Hodgins sold Resolved was Larrikin. I am told that Larrikin means "naughty" or "unruly lad" in Gaelic. If true, he sure lived up to his name. They couldn't even get him on the track, much less to the races, and finally Hodgins told Dad to get rid of him. Well, Dad liked him. Guess he liked a challenge.

The first thing Dad did was to take Larrikin to a friend's farm in adjoining Jessamine County and turn him out with three workhorses. He was left there until December, when it was cold and the snow was flying. Those workhorses must have beat the hell out of him. Dad took the van down to pick him up and said he darn near turned the van over getting into it. He wanted to get the hell out of there!

The second thing he did was to turn him over to a trainer friend, H.B. "Pappy" Pieratt. Pappy was a great guy. Called everybody John. I was John, Dad was John, anybody walked into his little bar in Lexington was John. Convenient. He was a barrel of fun, and I loved him.

Pappy fed the old horse peppermints and that, coupled with his workhorse experience, turned him around. He was never a sound horse, but Pappy did

Larrikin beating the classy stakes winners Dogoon and Solution at Keeneland on October 10, 1958. That's trainer H.B. "Pappy" Pieratt in cap and tie. *Track photographer, Keeneland Association.*

a great job getting him ready to run. His first start was at River Downs in a straight maiden race, and he won as far as you could throw a rock in 1:09 and change for six furlongs. He then went to Cleveland and won several handicaps at Thistledowns and Randall Park, tracks that were located right across the street from each other. Randall is a shopping center now, but Thistledowns thrives today. Larrikin's next stop was Keeneland, and then things really got exciting.

Pappy entered him in an allowance sprint, and the favorite in the race was a Dixiana filly named Fideles, trained by Hodgins. I was going back to the paddock to watch him saddle when I pretty near got run over by a friend, Pat Hillock. Pat was Larrikin's blacksmith. He also was the blacksmith for Calumet and had shod the likes of Citation, Coaltown and Ponder, to name a few. Pat was headed for the mutual windows but slowed down enough to say, "Ercel, this is like a license to steal." He was right. Larrikin was a come-from-behind sprinter, and he ran down Fideles to win by daylight. I think he paid something like four to one to win.

Later, at Keeneland, he beat really good stakes horses in a tough allowance test, coming from behind again to beat E. Gay Drake's Dogoon, a full brother to Swoon's Son, and the Dixiana bred Solution, setting a track record of 1:16 and 2/5 for six and a half furlongs. The old boy had talent.

Larrikin was owned by Dad, Harold Jordan and Pappy's son Frank. They paid the bills, Pappy did the training and a great time was had by all. When Larrikin's racing days were over, Dad leased a small farm on the east side of Lexington just to have a place for him to live out his days. When Dad passed away, I took over Larrikin's care for the last few years of his life. The blacksmith had trimmed him one morning, and when I returned to feed that afternoon, the old boy had somehow broken his shoulder and had to be put down. He's with Pappy and the boys now, but he had to leave me with one more bill to pay.

Little Priss produced one other foal of note, her first, a filly by Platter named Marie K. She never won and produced but one foal to earn blacktype. She was, however, the granddam of Grade 1 winner Habitony; graded stakes winner Kaye's Commander, a filly that also placed in the Kentucky Oaks; graded stakes winner Roman Numerals; and several other nice stakes winners. Blood will tell.

Platter also brings back memories. He won the 1944 Pimlico Futurity for George D. Widener and was at stud at Widener's Old Kenny Farm right next door to Dixiana. Eight Thirty also was at stud there. Both were chestnuts, but Eight Thirty was many lengths the better racehorse and a terrific sire. He was drop-dead gorgeous. The best thing Platter ever sired was Platan, winner of the Lawrence Realization and placed in a couple of other stakes. Eight Thirty, on the other hand, sired a long list of stakes winners, among them one that I have good reason to remember. That would be Lights Up, winner of the Travers in 1950. I didn't see the Travers, but I did see him win the Golden Gate Handicap in 1952. I had won a nice bet on him the week before when he upset a colt named Phil D. He was second choice to Phil D. in the Golden Gate Handicap the next week, and I cashed another ticket. Funny how you can recall the wins and not the losses. I was, and still am, a lousy handicapper. I just cashed those tickets because his daddy was a neighbor.

While I'm bragging about winning bets, I may as well bring up my one claim to handicapping fame. I was stationed in San Francisco and hitchhiked to Los Angeles to see the running of the 1952 Santa Anita Derby. Got there after the first race and picked six straight winners. Hill

Gail won the Santa Anita Derby at the expense of favored Windy City II, who, I recall, came out of the race sore. Had a heckuva time picking the sixth winner. Had it down to three horses and at the last second bet on a horse named The Driller. Never will forget that name. The Driller won in a three-horse photo, and I didn't have to hitchhike back to San Francisco. Flew back.

MISS TORO

(Daughter of Miss Jemima)

Another daughter of Miss Jemima was Miss Toro, a foal of 1932 by Toro, a son of The Porter. She won at two and three and produced two fine stakes winners, Sirocco and Four Winds. Sirocco was her first foal, Four Winds her fourth. Both were by Sweep All; in fact, her first five foals were all by Sweep All. Sirocco won the 1939 Walden Stakes in Maryland as a two-year-old, beating his stablemate Faymar, also by Sweep All, then won the Classic at Arlington, besting Kentucky Derby winner Gallahadion and Bimelech. He won by seven under George "The Iceman" Woolf. Awhile back, Barbara Livingston, a great photographer, posted a picture on Facebook of a horse taken during a breeze and asked if anyone could identify it. She had purchased a collection of photographs, and it was one of them. It was Sirocco. The picture was taken on the training track at Dixiana in the spring of 1940. He wintered in Kentucky and was getting ready for the Kentucky Derby, in which he ran fifth. I know that track like the back of my hand. I had walked that rail dozens of times as a kid, and there was a tunnel under that track to the infield, very handy during my courting days. Sirocco came to a tragic end, breaking a leg as a four-year-old.

Four Winds was a very, very talented filly. She was a bit of a disappointment as a producer but did throw Jet Stream, a Jet Pilot colt who placed in the San Marco Handicap, and the filly Laughing Breeze, a daughter of Windy City II who ran third in the 1963 Spinster at Keeneland (won by Lamb Chop).

Another daughter of Miss Toro was Kona Wind. A foal of 1941, she was a big chestnut, standing maybe 16.3 hands. At least she looked big to me. She was the first racehorse I ever hot walked. I must have been about twelve at the time. Maybe I should say that she hot walked me. She had a monster stride, and I had to darn near jog to keep up. But she was a sweetheart. Kona Wind never won stakes but did win seven races; however, she did not end up at Dixiana. She produced four winners and was granddam of two stakes winners, Red Bayou, winner of the Laurance Armour Handicap and third in the Stars and Stripes in Chicago, and Tito L., a stakes winner in Puerto Rico. I hope she had a good life.

Miss Toro's last foal arrived in 1951 and was named Blue Hawaii, by Polynesian, and I have good reason to remember her well. I spent the winter of 1955–56 with the Dixiana racing stable at the Fair Grounds in New Orleans. The trainer was Jack Hodgins, and he was a great lover of doing up horses in mud. I wound up with the softest hands in the South! Blue Hawaii was one of those done up regularly. One night we had a big-time rain and a portion of the barn flooded including Blue Hawaii's stall. She loved it. When we got to her, her bandages had slipped down because she had played around so much. I tucked away that little bit of knowledge, and it paid off. In the spring we moved to Keeneland and Hodgins entered her in a nice allowance race. Well, a couple of hours before post time, we had a downpour, and the track came up sloppy. Blue made three car payments for me.

Later that summer, Blue placed in a couple of nice stakes, the Modesty and the Honeymoon handicaps, and she was a nice producer at Dixiana. She was the dam of ten winners, including the stakes-winning filly Blade Away, by Blade, and two colts that placed in stakes.

Getting back to Sirocco, he and his stablemate, Faymar, ran one-two in the Walden Stakes as two-year-olds. Faymar came out of the race with a bowed tendon. He faced a bleak future, so Dad gave him to a foxhunting friend, George Gill, from Shelbyville. A couple of years later he bumped into Gill at a hunt. That old tendon had set and was as cold as ice. "Tried to buy him back, but George would have none of that. Told me he was the best horse he'd ever sat on." Dad was big into fox hunting.

We lived the first few years of my life on a piece of land on Iron Works Pike at the foot of where Kenny Lane empties onto Iron Works. It's still there, surrounded by Spendthrift Farm, but the house is gone. It was a two-story frame best described as a country farmhouse. Dad raised foxhounds, and I loved the dogs. Every morning, weather permitting, I would go out on the side porch and whistle; you could hear the puppies coming, and they would climb all over me. Heaven for a kid!

Sirocco, Arlington Classic winner, July 20, 1940, rider George Woolf. *C. Schultz, Arlington Park track photographer.*

Every fall, my parents would take my sister, Peggy, who was five years my senior, and me out of school, and we would go foxhunting in Estill County. We stayed at the home of a lovely couple, Jim May and Mabel Reeves. Great food. Feather beds. Wood-burning fireplaces. Swing on the front porch. Outside privy. Two-seater. No bath for three days. I loved it!

We would get up before dawn, have breakfast and pile in our cars and drive wherever we were going to cast the hounds, as they called it. They would turn some seventy-five to one hundred hounds loose, and riders would follow and judge them in various categories. I still have a fox horn a hound named Mata Hari won for endurance. Dad named the registered foxhounds after horses. There was Mata Hari, Top Flight, Singing Wood and another named Jean Harlow, which tells you something about Dad's taste in the ladies. After the hunt, I would take my horn behind the Reeves house, which was on a hill above Drowning Creek, and call the hounds home. They would come to the call.

Dad would often take several hounds to Estill County to hunt. He had an old truck that he converted into what he called the "dog wagon." This was back in the '30s, and the truck was old at the time. The route taken was the old Richmond Road then across the Kentucky River, over an old bridge at the bottom with steep hills on each side. He was coming home on one occasion and was about halfway down the hill when a wheel came bouncing by, headed straight for the river. It was the right rear wheel on the dog wagon, and the only thing to stop it from going in the river was a telephone pole. Well, it hit the pole dead center and bounced back onto the road. Dad climbed out, put the wheel back on, thanked the Lord and came on home.

4

Influential Dixiana Horses

WAR WOMAN

Wouldn't you know that the best runner bred by Mr. Fisher was out of a mare by Man o' War? That was War Woman, a foal of 1926. War Woman was unraced. So was her dam, Topaz, and her granddam and, for that matter, her great-granddam. You have to dig back a few generations to find a good horse in the pedigree, but he was a good one. That was Questionnaire, a son of Sting. Questionnaire won eighteen races, among them the Metropolitan and the Brooklyn Handicaps, and ran third in the 1930 Belmont Stakes to Gallant Fox and Whichone. He was successful at stud. Still, War Woman had a weak female family. Her pedigree was pretty typical of the quality of mares bred to Man o' War. Didn't make any difference. In 1930, she was bred to the unraced stallion Peter Hastings, who was turned out at the farm, and in 1931 she produced Mata Hari, champion two-year-old filly of 1933.

War Woman had been scheduled to be bred that year to a stallion standing at Idle Hour Farm, likely North Star III, because Dixiana sent Miss Jemima to North Star III that year. War Woman had a mind of her own. For two days she refused to be loaded for the trip to Idle Hour. Finally, they gave up. Ross Long, the Dixiana manager at the time, told the groom, "Go get Peter Hastings." The result was Mata Hari. One of those scientific matings.

Peter Hastings was out of a mare by Hastings, which meant that the resulting foal, Mata Hari, was inbred 3×3 to Hastings. Now, that's a recipe for trouble! Mata Hari was to pull this same stunt by refusing to load a few years later—only her refusal came after she had been covered by the stallion. The result of that episode was that she was hand walked home, a distance of at least fifteen miles. Peter Hastings sired one other stakes winner, a minor one named Chigre, and ended up with the remount service in Michigan.

Peter Hastings also was the sire of Petrose, the sire of the high-class runner Pet Bully. Like his sire, Petrose was unraced. Since the 1947 sale of a part of Dixiana, ownership of that section had changed several times. Pet Bully was at stud when it was owned by Howard Reineman and known as Crown Crest Farm, and Pet Bully is buried there. William Shively has since put together much of the old Dixiana, including that section. Also buried there are Oil Capital, a stablemate of Pet Bully at Crown Crest, and the stallions Grey Dawn II, Al Hattab and Dewan. The latter three, all successful at stud, were there when the property was owned and operated by Jimmy Drymon and called Domino Stud.

One of my favorite research sources is *A Quarter Century of American Racing*, the Silver Anniversary Supplement to the *Blood-Horse* published on August 30, 1941. Over the years, I have just about memorized the whole thing, without paying much attention to the advertising within. I should have. You can learn a lot from that, too. A short while back, I happened to glance at an ad featuring six stallions standing at Valdina Farms, Sabinal, Texas. Lo and behold, there was Petrose. Now, Pet Bully wasn't foaled until seven years after the book came off the presses, and he didn't win a stakes until he was a four-year-old, but he won a passel of them after that, eleven in all. He won the Phoenix Handicap at Keeneland as a five-year-old, beating Calumet's Hill Gail for owner Ada L. Rice, who, with husband Dan, operated Danada Farm. Pet Bully's dam was the unraced Bull Dog mare Camelina. Camelina produced eleven foals, and the last four were by stallions standing at Danada: Olympia, King of the Tutors, Vertex and Nilo. Vertex was one of my favorites, a gorgeous liver chestnut and a flat runner. He was a member of the same crop as Bold Ruler, Round Table, Gallant Man and, at one stage of his career, was considered to be the best handicap horse in the East. Round Table was the best in the West and in the nation at the same time. Vertex also was successful at stud, siring, among others, Kentucky Derby winner Lucky Debonair. I am pretty sure that Pet Bully was not named by the folks at Valdina Farm. They had the unfortunate habit of naming their horses Valdina this and Valdina that.

War Woman produced three other foals that won, but nothing else of note. Mata Hari, however, was the dam of a colt, Spy Song, that ran second in the Kentucky Derby, and she was granddam of several other stakes winners. Blacktype was on the top of her pedigree, and there was an abundance of it.

Mata Hari was, of course, retired to the broodmare band at Dixiana and was bred several times to Balladier, a son of Black Toney standing at Patchen Wilkes Farm on Winchester Road east of Lexington. Now, during her breeding career, Mata Hari—we all called her Mat—produced four foals to Balladier's cover, but on this occasion, she decided she was going to stay at Patchen Wilkes. It was a big mistake to get into an argument with Mat, as many an assistant starter had discovered. Jack Delzel, who worked for Dixiana, mostly with the show horses, had vanned her over to Patchen Wilkes, and after several hours of coaxing, cajoling, bribing and praying he gave up. "To hell with it, I'm going to walk her home." Now that fifteen-mile estimate is a conservative one, but they made it. Mat had never pulled a stunt like that before and never did again.

Jack Delzel was a great guy. He started out working with show horses at Dixiana but moved to the Thoroughbred division when the show horses were sold in a dispersal in 1947. He was with General George Patton in World War II, and he and my mother corresponded. I remember he wrote in one letter about Patton that "this crazy bastard is going to get me killed."

I used to hang out at the show horse barn when I was a kid because of Jack Delzel. One day, I had my Red Ryder BB gun with me, and Jack stuck a match in the ground. "Here kid, let's see you light this match." Now I knew that my chances of doing that were slim to none, so I shot from the hip. Proof. There stood the match, burning away. I'll never forget the expression on Jack's face! I was smart enough to walk away before he asked me to do it again.

After the war, Delzel went back to work at Dixiana, this time traveling with the racing stable trained by Jack Hodgins. He stayed with Hodgins for several years, then went with Mac Miller as assistant trainer. He turned down many training jobs, saying he didn't want all the responsibility and the headaches that came with it. At one time, he was asked to take care of two particular horses that needed special care, and Miller loaned him out. The two were champion two-year-old Hoist the Flag, who was injured after staying undefeated in his two starts as a three-year-old, winning an allowance race at Bowie and the Bay Shore at Aqueduct, and Kentucky Derby winner Canonero II. When Jack Delzel passed away Mac Miller put up a marker for him in the centerfield of the training track at Aiken, South Carolina.

MATA HARI

Other than a strong will to do it her way, Mata Hari did not have a mean bone in her body. Once she decided that enough was enough, it was best just to leave her alone. I had the privilege of cleaning her stall and turning her out dozens of times, with and without a foal at her side. She was a good mama. Her first foals, and I do mean foals, arrived in 1935—twins, neither of which survived. Her first live foal, a colt by Sickle, arrived in 1936. Mary Fisher named him What Now. What now indeed. He won nine races. Two years later, it was Wiretapper, by Ksar, and he won five times. Spy Snare, a colt by Questionnaire, was next, and that was an interesting mating. Mat's third dam was a half sister to the dam of Questionnaire. It was not a strong female family—you had to go back to Mat's third dam to find blacktype.

Mat produced four foals by Balladier. The first, Singing Spy, died before starting. The second was a filly named Sub Rosa. She, too, was unraced, but she became the dam of the good stakes winner Sub Fleet, by Count Fleet.

Mata Hari, champion two-year-old filly of 1933. *"Skeets" Meadows, photographer.*

Sub Rosa also was the dam of Wondring, a daughter of Pensive; Wondring won the Ashland Stakes and ran second in the 1950 Kentucky Oaks. Sub Fleet ran a mile and a quarter in track record time of 2:00 and 3/5 to win the Hawthorne Gold Cup, won the Kentucky Jockey Club Stakes and Sheridan Handicap and placed in a bunch of stakes, among them a second to Hill Gail in the 1952 Kentucky Derby.

The third Balladier foal from Mat was Spy Song. He made his first start at the old Lincoln Fields track in Chicago, going four and a half furlongs and set a new track record to win by twelve. Moving to Washington Park, he won his second start and made hash of his field that day, too. His third outing was in the Arlington Futurity. It was pouring rain, so much you could barely distinguish the horses down the backstretch. All you could determine was that there was one horse way in front of the field, but you couldn't make out who it was until inside the sixteenth pole. It was Spy Song. His fourth start was in the Washington Park Futurity, and here misfortune caught up with him. He was kicked in the knee at the post and was through for the season.

The fourth foal by Balladier out of Mata Hari was Mr. Music. He got shipping fever, which affected his breathing, and did not race, but he became a very useful sire, first at Dixiana, then at Pharamond Farm in Michigan, owned by Mr. Fisher's daughter-in-law, Susan. He sired a really nice stakes winner for George D. Widener named Seven Thirty and several other good stakes winners.

The next-to-last foal out of Mat was Spy Defense, a Bull Lea colt that placed in several stakes, and her last was the 1951 Roman colt named Roman Spy, winner of forty-five races, including the Motor City Handicap. Mat died shortly thereafter, tough to the end. Dad said she died on her feet, refusing to go down. I was away, in the service, at the time. Glad I wasn't there.

Balladier was one of the best two-year-olds of 1934, winning the Champagne Stakes and the United States Hotel Stakes, beating Omaha, the next year's Triple Crown winner, in both events. He was injured in the Futurity and never raced again. Bradley already had an abundance of that particular sire line at Idle Hour, so he offered Joe Goodwin, owner of Patchen Wilkes Farm, his choice of Balladier or Blue Larkspur. Goodwin chose Balladier because he was the younger of the two. Besides Spy Song, Balladier was the sire of Double Jay, Kentucky Colonel and Papa Redbird. Spy Song did very well at stud at Dixiana, and Kentucky Colonel and Papa Redbird were useful sires at Patchen Wilkes. Double Jay was by far the most successful at stud. He stood at Claiborne Farm, and Abe Hewitt related this story in his book *Sire Lines*, published by the *Blood-Horse*, as told to him by A.B. Bull Hancock Jr:

> *Double Jay was trained by Duke McCue…and Duke was a wild man if ever there was one. I happened to be in the secretary's office when Duke came in to make his entry for Double Jay in the Kentucky Jockey Club Stakes. Everybody was kidding him and Duke couldn't take kidding. Somebody said, "Duke, what the hell are you putting that damn horse in there for? You should have left him in New Jersey. Education will top him out at the gate and open up so far you'll never catch him, not even if they go around twice."*
>
> *Well, Duke just went crazy. He reached into his pocket and pulled out eight $100 bills. "My horse will be in front of Education at every pole," he said, "any pole he's not, you win a hundred and any pole he is, I win the hundred." So they covered him and I went back to the races the next day. I thought no horse in the world could top Education, and if it did I didn't think it possible they could stay a mile. That sucker Double Jay topped him and won it. So I made up my mind right then and there that I wanted to stand that horse.*

Double Jay stood at Claiborne Farm for twenty-two seasons, ranked among the leading sires eight times and was twice the nation's leading broodmare sire. Hancock didn't make many mistakes in the horse business, especially when selecting stallions to stand at Claiborne.

SPY SONG

Spy Song, a foal of 1943 by Balladier out of Mata Hari, was a grand-looking horse. He was brown with a star and stood 16.1 hands. Very correct, and to this day, I have not seen a quicker horse out of the starting gate. He would make a good start look bad. Dad would get calls from quarter horse breeders wanting to send mares to him. I did see him break poorly on one occasion. Dad had taken me with him to see the 1946 running of the American Derby. When they threw the latch, Spy Song was taking a step backward, and he broke absolutely last. The race was at a mile and an eighth, which meant that the first eighth of a mile was at the finish line and right in front of the grandstand. Spy Song came rolling out, hit Revoked

Spy Song winning at Arlington Park in 1947. Note how high he carries his head. *Arlington Park, track photographer.*

and turned him sideways and had a daylight lead after the first eighth of a mile. You could hear the crowd gasp, but it was all to no avail. He ended up out of the money.

Spy Song was a sprinter. He had a habit of carrying his head high when he ran, which was not uncommon in horses with Man o' War's blood. This was really noticeable in the grand stayer Stymie, who was inbred 3x3 to Man o' War. Spy Song did manage to run a pacesetting second in the Kentucky Derby to Triple Crown winner Assault, but he was a well-beaten second. Assault won by eight. Actually, Spy Song was lucky to be second. Third, beaten a head for second money, was Foxcatcher Farm's Hampden. Hampden's rider misjudged the finish line and stood up at the sixteenth pole, a mistake duplicated by Bill Shoemaker eleven years later on Gallant Man.

I know that Dad made money on the Derby that day. There was another speed horse in the race named Rippey, a son of Stimulus, owned by William Helis. Dad had a bet with a Rippey fan with only the two involved like a match race. Whichever was in front at each pole earned five dollars. Spy Song took the lead out of the gate and was in front deep into the stretch with only Assault passing him. With ten poles involved, Dad won fifty dollars. That would buy a lot of mint juleps in 1946.

After the defeat in the American Derby, Spy Song was usually kept in sprints, although he did finish second in the ten-furlong Hawthorne Derby. They would run sprint stakes in Chicago every couple of weeks that would draw fields consisting of speed horses like Spy Song, Rippey, With Pleasure, Inroc and occasionally Armed. The racing secretary would juggle the weights to, in theory at least, even things out. Spy Song won five of them.

Spy Song was retired to Dixiana and his stud fee was $3,500. Later, after his first crop came out running, it was up to $5,000 and his book was limited to thirty-five mares. The best thing he ever sired was Crimson King Farm's Crimson Satan, the champion two-year-old of 1961. Crimson Satan was a chestnut out of Papila, a mare that had placed in the Chilian Oaks. Somewhere, tucked away in a sometimes-faulty memory, is that veterinarian Arnold Pessin had found the mare for Peter Salmen, owner of Crimson King Farm, and I believe he got her from Jack Price, breeder, owner and trainer of Carry Back. Peter Salmen Jr., son of the owner, said that they had sent Papila to Spy Song on my recommendation. I sure don't remember that, but I'm glad to take credit. Crimson Satan won $797,077 for the Salmens and was retired to stud at Gainesway Farm, where he did quite well.

A couple of years ago, there was a celebration of Man o' War's 100th birthday. They had a big display of Man o' War pictures at the Keeneland library. Of course, I had to go check it out. When I walked in, the first thing I saw was a head shot of Spy Song. I asked, "Why the picture of Spy Song?" The reply was that they had found the picture with the collection of Man o' War photographs and had a difficult time identifying it. Being a wise guy, I asked, "Why didn't you call me? But leave it up, Spy Song's second dam was War Woman, by Man o' War."

Spy Song was a very kind horse, easy to handle, and Dad loved him. There is no marker, but he's buried behind the stud barn at Dixiana.

THE KNITTER

The Knitter was not a typical High Time, even though she was a chestnut. She didn't win in three starts as a two-year-old as 57 percent of the High Times did, but she produced the winners of seventy-four races for Dixiana. The best were Red Cross, a filly by War Jeep that ran second in the Arlington Lassie Stakes and third in the Princess Pat, the latter at the old Washington Park in Chicago; Whitleather, a colt by Unbreakable that placed in the Chagrin Valley Turf Stakes; and Safe Message, a colt by Spy Song that won twenty-two races, including the 1959 Ben Ali Handicap at Keeneland.

Safe Message was one tough nut, in more ways than one. I spent the winter of 1956–57 with the Dixiana racing stable at Gulfstream, and one of my duties was to hold the horses while their winter coats were being clipped. We had put cotton in Safe Message's ears to muffle the sound of the clippers, and when we reached up to take it out, he went straight up and came down on me with the leg over the twitch. Cuts and bruises, especially to the ego. A bit of the Mata Hari in his pedigree, I assume. Anyway, we both recovered nicely. I was in the paddock prior to his win in the Ben Ali at Keeneland. The trainer, Jack Hodgins, was approached by a gentleman, I think it was Hal Bishop, who wanted to buy Safe Message and asked how much. Hodgins replied, "$50,000, and you will give it to me after this race." Safe Message went out and won a three-horse photo over Ezgo and Shan Pac and found a new home.

The Knitter's dam was the good winner Penelope, by Sweep, and Penelope produced two stakes winners for Dixiana, Shiny Penny and Constant Wife. Shiny Penny, by Torchilla, won twenty-five races, among them three stakes with placings in four more. Constant Wife was by Chicle and one of three stakes-winning fillies from Dixiana's foal crop of 1931. The other two were Mata Hari and Far Star. Constant Wife won the Hialeah Juvenile Championship Stakes and ran second to Far Star in the Debutante.

Another foal out of The Knitter was Penroyal, an unraced daughter of Royal Minstrel. Penroyal's first two foals were nothing to call home about, and she was given away to a friend of my dad's, Tilford Wilson, owner of Wilson Machinery Company in Lexington, and Carl Houston. Well, Penroyal proceeded to produce four high-class stakes winners for her new owners in Royal Note, Royal Mustang, Great Dream and Phar Mon.

Royal Note was by Spy Song, and as a two-year-old in 1954, he won the Arlington Futurity, Bashford Manor Stakes, Dover Stakes, Cherry Hill Stakes, the Lafayette, equaled the track record over the Headley course at Keeneland and set a new track record of :34 flat at Oaklawn. Royal Note beat Nashua in the Cherry Hill, and when he was retired to stud, his owners used to advertise him as the only horse of Nashua's age to give him weight and beat him. He went to stud at Joe Metz's Farm on Shannon Run Road.

Royal Mustang was by Easy Mon. He won the Stars and Stripes Handicap in Chicago and placed in thirteen other stakes, among them a second to Count Turf in the 1951 Kentucky Derby, a second in the Blue Grass Stakes and a second in the 1950 Breeders Futurity.

Great Dreams was a filly by Grey Dream, a son of imported Gino that ended up at stud in Nebraska, where he was quite popular. Sired a lot of winners. Great Dream won three stakes on the West Coast and later produced a couple of runners that placed in stakes.

Phar Mon, a full brother by Easy Mon to Royal Mustang, won the Bashford Manor Stakes at Churchill, the Lafayette Stakes at Keeneland and the Hialeah Juvenile Stakes as a two-year-old in 1949.

So, The Knitter, by High Time out of Penelope, had a license to be a good producer, and she was.

Getting back to Royal Note, in the spring of 1959, I rode out with Dad to take a look at a yearling filly owned by T. Owen Campbell of Lexington. His farm was on the Winchester Pike just past Hamburg Place. As I recall, the filly was a medium-sized bay, rather plain, but with no obvious faults. The groom showing the filly said, "Here's the one you should take a look at," and led out a good-size filly, a dark bay, and she was impressive. "She's by Royal Note," we were informed. Well, that was Little Tumbler, and the following year she defeated colts to win the Futurity, beating Globemaster and Garwol, two colts that went on to win major stakes. Little Tumbler also won the Astoria and the Colleen Stakes, and I got to see her win the Alcibiades at Keeneland, besting Times Two and Bright Silver. She was owned by Bruno Ferrari, trained by W.R. Mitchell and ridden by Ray Broussard that day. Later in her career she set a new track record at Aqueduct going six and a half furlongs but never won another stakes after her two-year-old season. As a broodmare, she was dam of Native Tumbler, a Native Dancer filly that won stakes, and was the granddam of several other stakes winners.

FULMAR

Fulmar was a foal of 1941 by Hairan out of Saramar, by High Time. She won eight times for Dixiana, mostly in allowance company and was often used as a workhorse for Spy Song by her trainer, Jack Hodgins. She had an abundance of speed, and they would break her off several lengths in front of Spy Song to give him something to run at. I recall Hodgins remarking, "I probably didn't do right by that filly, but she was the only thing in the stable with enough speed to go with Spy Song." Well, he sure didn't hurt her as a broodmare. Fulmar later produced two stakes winners by Spy Song: Fulvous and Fulcrum. Dig back in the pedigree of Fulmar, and you'll find one of the all-time great speed sires, Ariel. Ariel stood at Walter Salmon's Mereworth Farm.

Hodgins had been an assistant starter when Mata Hari was racing. He survived that and went on to train Mata Hari's best son, Spy Song, and later Fulvous, a filly from the first crop by Spy Song and his first stakes winner.

Fulvous was a medium-sized chestnut with the stable name of "Pinkie." Never did know why they gave her that handle. She was a foal of 1950, and I was working for Uncle Sam at the time she went into training. She won the two big stakes for juvenile fillies in Chicago, the Arlington Lassie and the Princess Pat, giving Spy Song a great start at stud. Later, she produced stakes winner Goldflower, a filly by Greek Song better known around the barn as Frances, a nickname acquired because of her flop years. There was a TV show at the time about a mule called "Francis, the talking mule." A real classic.

Goldflower arrived in 1958, and she won the Ashland Stakes and the Modesty Handicap. After a couple of barren years, Fulvous produced Golden Ruler, a colt by King of the Tudors. King of the Tudors was standing at Danada Farm. Golden Ruler won the Arlington Washington Futurity and was trained by Chuck Wertsler. He had shelly feet and didn't go on after his stakes win. I remember he lost a shoe in the paddock prior to the start of the Futurity and a blacksmith had to reset it. But he won.

Fulcrum, a full brother to Fulvous, loved Keeneland. He won the 1957 running of the Breeders' Futurity, then came back as a five-year-old to win the Ben Ali Handicap in an upset over the heavy favorite, Dunce, son of Tom Fool. Dunce had won both the American Derby and Arlington Classic. A friend of mine, Bud Wallace, who was advertising manager of the *Thoroughbred Record* and author of a column that appeared regularly in the *Lexington Herald*, had a wad of tickets on Dunce that would choke a horse. Three years earlier, Fulcrum had cost him a big score in the Breeders' Futurity. Throwing his tickets in the air, he stepped out of the press box, saying some not very nice things about Fulcrum. In addition to winning the Breeders' Futurity and the Ben Ali, Fulcrum set two records at Keeneland, six furlongs in 1:08 and 4/5 and the about seven furlongs of the Beard Course in 1:25 and 2/5. He was given an opportunity at stud but received little patronage.

Another daughter of Fulvous was Fulgent, by Spy Song. She won only one race, but she was the dam of the stakes winner Beauful, a filly by Beau Gar that was trained by Alan Jerkens. Beauful won the Bed o' Roses Handicap and the Hannah Dustin Handicap and equaled the track record at Aqueduct for six furlongs, 1:08 and 3/5. Fulgent was also the dam of Gray Slacks, a filly by Native Dancer that won the Vagrancy in 1969.

Getting back to Golden Ruler, he went to stud at Dixiana and sired one of my all-time favorite horses, Hard Work. Hard Work was a grand-looking chestnut colt. He stood about 16.2 with a great shoulder and had talent. He won the Breeders Futurity at Keeneland and set a new track record over the Beard Course but developed a blood disorder and darn near died. He went home to stud at Dixiana and became a poor man's dream sire. I bred to him as often as I could; he stood for a fee of $1,000, and I got some very useful runners by him. The best was a colt named Elbow Grease, and two other Hard Works that I bred placed in stakes.

I didn't name Elbow Grease. I sold him at Keeneland in the fall for, as I recall, $13,700, and why he brought that much I'll never know. He was downright homely. We called him Moose. Big jughead. He was a red chestnut with more white on him than a Hereford steer. A fellow named Manfred Roos bought him, and Roos was a better judge of the horse than I because Moose could run. Jackie and I went to Turfway to watch him run in the Forego Stakes, and he ran a credible fourth. His next start was at Keeneland in an allowance race, and he finished in about the middle of the pack. I went to the paddock to take a look before the race, and his looks hadn't improved.

Roos was from New England and he took Moose to Suffolk Downs. This was back when racing at Suffolk was pretty strong and they ran a stakes just about every Saturday. The purses were not that big, but a dollar was worth a lot more then than it is now. Moose knocked off several stakes, set a new track record for five and a half furlongs on the grass, and earned right at $200,000. Pretty is as pretty does, I guess.

5

Forgotten Champions

TOP FLIGHT

There was no question as to who was the champion two-year-old of 1931. It was C.V. Whitney's unbeaten filly Top Flight, a daughter of imported Disc Donc and the five-time winner Flyatit, by Peter Pan. She was bred by Harry Payne Whitney, who passed away in 1930, and raced in his son's colors. Top Flight was dark brown with a blaze face and white stockings that extended halfway up the cannon bone behind. She started seven times as a two-year-old, all seven in stakes, and won them all, beating colts in the Saratoga Special, the Futurity and the Pimlico Futurity. While there were no polls as such then, she was considered the best two-year-old of the year. Joe Palmer, in *A Quarter Century of American Racing*, listed her at the top over both colts and fillies. Good enough for me.

Top Flight began her two-year-old year with a win in the Clover Stakes at Aqueduct on June 17, 1931. Trainer Thomas Healy then took her to Chicago, where she won the Lassie Stakes with ease, then to Saratoga for wins over colts in the Saratoga Special and another easy score over her own sex in the Spinaway. Moving to Belmont for her next two starts, she won the Matron Stakes, then the seven-furlong Futurity, both down the straightaway on the Widener Chute. Her last start of the year was her first around two turns in the mile and a sixteenth Pimlico Futurity, and she won by a neck over Tick On and the next year's Kentucky

Derby winner Burgoo King, a colt by Bubbling Over bred and owned by Colonel E.R. Bradley.

Top Flight's first start as a three-year-old was an ambitious one against colts in the Wood Memorial, and she tired to finish fourth. Back against fillies, she reeled off wins in the Acorn, the Coaching Club American Oaks and the Arlington Oaks before trying the boys again. This time it was in the Classic at Arlington Park won by the high-class Gusto, a colt by American Flag; Gusto also won the American Derby and the Jockey Club Gold Cup that year. Next time out, Top Flight easily won the Alabama Stakes, going a mile and a quarter, then took on older males in the Delaware Handicap at Saratoga, not to be confused with the Delaware Handicap for fillies and mares run, as you might expect, at Delaware Park. She was in over her head again and ran fourth, beaten five lengths by Flagstone, a year her elder and a son of Sun Flag, by Sun Briar. Flagstone's half sister was High Maria, a filly by High Time that won the Jeanne d'Arc Stakes.

Back against fillies in her next outing, Top Flight won the Lady's Handicap at Belmont. Then, on September 24, in what was to be the last start of her career, she tried males one more time in the Potomac Handicap at Havre de Grace. She finished fourth, beaten two lengths by Dark Secret, Osculator and Gallant Sir. No disgrace there. Dark Secret, a roan colt by Flying Ebony, bred by Gifford A. Cochran, in the following year ranked second only to Equipoise among handicap horses, with Gallant Sir and Osculator also highly ranked. Ranked second only to Equipoise again in 1934, Dark Secret, at career's end, had won twenty-three times, fifteen stakes, including the Jockey Club Gold Cup twice, the Saratoga Cup, Manhattan Handicap and the Brooklyn Handicap.

Top Flight, retired to C.V. Whitney's broodmare band, produced one stakes winner. Her second foal was a colt by Peace Chance named Flight Command, and he won the United States Hotel Stakes as a two-year-old at Saratoga. Top Flight was the dam of White Lady, a daughter of the Whitney stallion Mahmoud; White Lady won and produced the good filly Snow White, winner of the filly division of the National Stallion Stakes and second in the 1948 running of the Alabama. Top Flight died in 1949 and is buried on property that is now Gainesway Farm.

TWENTY GRAND AND EQUIPOISE

Twenty Grand, winner of the 1931 Kentucky Derby, was one of the most popular horses of his time. There was even a popular brand of cigarettes named Twenty Grand. I remember puffing away on a Twenty Grand with my buddy Lou, whose dad owned the Jot 'Em Down Store. We were in a treehouse just down the hill. We were about ten or eleven at the time with our Twenty Grands and a Grapette and watched the cars go by. Twenty Grand cigarettes have faded into obscurity. So have the Grapettes for that matter. But the horse still lives with many of us.

Twenty Grand was a foal of 1928 by St. Germans out of Bonus, by All Gold, and he was bred and owned by Greentree Farm. Bonus was blind, and her foals wore a bell so she would know they were nearby. Twenty Grand was the heavy favorite for the Derby, and he ran like it, winning by four lengths over Dixiana's Sweep All with Preakness winner Mate third three lengths behind Sweep All. Mate had won the Preakness run for the eleventh and last time before the Derby. Twenty Grand set a new track record in the Derby, 2:01 and 4/5, which stood until Whirlaway bettered it in 1941. Sweep All had taken a lead a mile into the race but couldn't withstand the run by Twenty Grand. This prompted J.A. "Joe" Estes to write this poem about Sweep All. It appeared in the May 30, 1931 edition of the *Blood-Horse*:

Sweep All, to Himself
At the Post

"Too small a hoss," I heard 'em say.
"And too much Sweep. He'll never stay.
Before they're half a mile away
He'll have the white flag showing."
It makes me mad to hear 'em squall
Like that as if they knew it all.
Come on, hoss, line up in that stall,
Let's get this Derby going.

The Start

The barrier's up. You'll need no whip
To goad me, jock. I'll hit a clip
To make the saddle strain and slip

And hosses' tongues hang out.
I see a green-and-white-hooped shirt
Ahead; and kicking up the dirt,
That grey streak makes a mighty spurt…
Ah, how they scream and shout!

THE BACKSTRETCH

I'm lying third. The sprinters fail.
Another speedster takes the trail.
A moment more, he flicks his tail
And is swallowed up in the field.
Now the sprinters are done, the stayers can do.
I'm ready now, I'm coming through.
What are they saying, all that crew
That knew how soon I'd yield!

TURNING FOR HOME

Well, here we are. The way is clear.
How sweet a tune it is to hear
A Derby's hoofbeats in the rear
And a clamoring crowd ahead.
And all that said my speed would die,
That knew I'd stop, and could tell you why,
I want to look 'em in the eye
And see 'em turning red.

THE FINISH

I think I'll run away and hide…
But what's this running at my side,
With superequine strength and stride
That leaps along the land?
He's a length ahead, now two, now four.
I'm beat. The winner's fame will soar…
It's honor enough for me, and more,
It took a Twenty Grand.

As good as he was, there is no doubt that Twenty Grand benefited from the absence of Equipoise, his stiff rival the previous year. The two met for three times as two-year-olds and each encounter was a dogfight. Twenty Grand beat Equipoise by a length in the Junior Champion Stakes at Aqueduct. Twelve days later, the margin was a nose in the Kentucky Jockey Club Stakes at Churchill, with Twenty Grand getting the nod. The two met again nineteen days later in the Pimlico Futurity, and this time Equipoise prevailed by a half length. In his final start at two, Twenty Grand ran third to Mate and Sweep All in the Walden Stakes at Pimlico. This was before the Experimental Free Handicap was established, and there was no polling as such. Joe Palmer, in the *Blood-Horse* publication *A Quarter Century of American Racing*, listed Equipoise, Twenty Grand, Jamestown and Mate in that order. Joe was seldom wrong.

Twenty Grand opened his three-year-old season with a win in the Wood Memorial. That was on May 2, and a week later he was blocked while making a strong move and was beaten a length and a half by Mate in the Preakness. Equipoise, who had terrible feet, had gone into the race with a quarter crack. He finished a well-beaten fourth and came out of the race lame and was through for the year.

Twenty Grand's next race after the Derby was the Belmont and he won by ten, beating Sun Meadow and Jamestown. Then three weeks later, he had another easy score in the Dwyer. Sent to Arlington, Twenty Grand ran a closing third to Mate and Spanish Play in the Classic. Mate, by Prince Pal, was retired to stud at John Wesley Marrs Clarkland Farm on the Brian Station Pike.

After the Classic, Twenty Grand rolled up four straight wins. He won the Travers, beat Sun Beau by ten lengths in the Saratoga Gold Cup, the Lawrence Realization by six, the Jockey Club Gold Cup by three. On October 5, 1932, he finished second in a handicap at Laurel and pulled up lame.

Twenty Grand was retired to stud at Greentree Farm and proved to be completely sterile. The St. Germans curse. He was put back in training and sent to California to prepare for the first running of the Santa Anita Handicap, the first race with a purse of $100,000 ever offered in North America. On January 25, 1935, some two years and four months after he had pulled up lame at Laurel, he ran third in a handicap at Santa Anita and pulled up lame again. In his next start, he hooked his old rival Equipoise in an overnight handicap. Twenty Grand won, but it was a battle, with Equipoise prevailing by a length only to be disqualified and placed second.

Five days later, both Equipoise and Twenty Grand finished out of the money in the Santa Anita Handicap, won by the Irish-bred Azucar.

Later that spring, Twenty Grand was sent to England, where he ran twice and got nothing. Returned home, he was retired to the "Gas House Gang." The Gas House Gang was the nickname given a group of retired horses by farmhands who were fans of the 1934 St. Louis Cardinals baseball team. The other members were Jolly Roger, a former champion steeplechaser; Easter Hero, who had raced over fences in England; and stakes winner Cherry Pie. Twenty Grand died at Greentree at age twenty.

Equipoise

The Santa Anita Handicap was the final start for Equipoise. He had been popular with racing fans and had been dubbed the Chocolate Soldier because of his color. He was a liver chestnut, which is a dark, rich, chocolate-brown coat. Equipoise carried the silks of C.V. Whitney, who had inherited him upon the death of his father, H.P. Whitney, and he was retired to stud at his owner's farm just north of Lexington. The land is now a part of Gainesway Farm, and Equipoise is buried there. He died at the age of ten in 1938, when his first foals were two-year-olds.

At first, it seemed that he was not destined to be successful at stud, but that changed with the arrival of the 1942 Kentucky Derby winner Shut Out, the superb Cup horse Bolingbroke, Coaching Club American Oaks winner Level Best and such high-class handicappers as Equity Fox, Attention and Swing and Sway, the latter the grandsire of 1961 Kentucky Derby winner Carry Back. Another son of Equipoise, the King Ranch stallion Equestrian, was the sire of one of the best handicappers of the 1940s, Stymie. Equipoise was also broodmare sire of the 1946 Triple Crown winner Assault. Equipoise was by Pennant, so he traced in tale male to Domino, a sire line whose survival today is tenuous at best.

Equipoise had not spent much time in his stall as a two-year-old. He started sixteen times, beginning in Maryland on April 7 with an easy win going a half mile on a track labeled heavy. He won again, then was third in the Aberdeen Stakes at Havre de Grace and came out of the race with a quarter crack. He stumbled at the start and unseated his rider in his next outing, then finished first in the Youthful at Jamaica only to be disqualified and placed second. That was the first of three disqualifications handed Equipoise during his career, events that prompted his regular rider, Sonny

Workman, to take several unscheduled vacations. Not that Workman was at fault. If Equipoise was blocked and it seemed that there was no hole to run through, by golly, Equipoise was going to make one!

After the Youthful, he reeled off four straight wins, taking the Keene Memorial, the Juvenile, the National Stallion and the American Stakes in New York before losing by a head to Jamestown after a troubled trip in the Saratoga Special. After winning the Eastern Shore Stakes at Havre de Grace, he hooked up with the first of his three duels with Twenty Grand.

Equipoise made but three starts as a three-year-old. He won the first, going six furlongs at Havre de Grace. In his second, also at Havre de Grace, he ran sixth, beaten over thirteen lengths and came out of the race with a quarter crack. Two weeks later, he ran fourth to Mate, Twenty Grand and Ladder in the Preakness and was through for the year.

Equipoise returned with a bang in 1932, winning his first seven starts and ending the season with ten wins, two seconds and a third in fourteen starts. Only once did he throw in a bad race, that in an overnight handicap at Havre de Grace going six furlongs when he ran fifth, beaten by nine lengths. As the old song goes, "fools can explain it, wise men never try."

He began his four-year-old season at Bowie, winning a five-furlong overnight followed with a three-length win in the Hartford Handicap going six furlongs at Havre de Grace. Thereafter, he was usually required to give weight to his opponents. Moving to Belmont, he picked up 129 pounds, giving the second-place runner 21 pounds, and won by a length. The Metropolitan was next, and he won by two and a half lengths, giving the second-place horse 9 pounds, then went to Arlington to run a mile in 1:34 and 2/5 under 128 to beat Jamestown, no easy feat, under 118. He made three more starts at Arlington, winning the nine-furlong Stars and Stripes carrying 129 and beating Tred Avon (107), the ten-furlong Arlington Gold Cup carrying 126 over Gusto (114), then lost for the first time that year when he was beaten by a neck in the ten-furlong Arlington Handicap to Plucky Play (111) while carrying 134. He next won back-to-back stakes at Saratoga, the Wilson and the Whitney, with similar ease with 126 pounds in each. Then Equipoise threw in a clunker at Havre de Grace followed with the win in the Havre de Grace Cup under 129, beating Gallant Sir (108). His final two starts of the year resulted in defeats, both at Laurel. He was third carrying 126 in the Laurel Stakes to Jack High (118) and Gallant Sir (108), then failed to give Tred Avon 17 pounds and was beaten by a head in the Washington Handicap. Third that day under 112 was his old rival, Mate.

Equipoise started his five-year-old season in the same manner as he had the year before by winning his first seven starts, and he ended it in the same manner by losing his last two. He began with a win in the Philadelphia Handicap, then won the Metropolitan, Suburban, Arlington Handicap, Wilson Stakes, Hawthorne Gold Cup and the Saratoga Cup going a mile and three quarters. He won the Suburban under 132 pounds and the Arlington Handicap under 135, giving great chunks of weight to all. In his final two starts of the year, he ran a poor third to Dark Secret and Gusto at equal weights in the Jockey Club Gold Cup then failed by a length under 132 to Osculator under 104 in the Havre de Grace Handicap. Mate (110) ran third.

Equipoise ran six times as a six-year-old in 1934 under weights varying from 130 to 134. He began by winning the Philadelphia and Dixie Handicaps then finished first in the Metropolitan only to be disqualified and placed second to Mr. Khayyam. In his last three races, he failed to give Ladysman 20 pounds and was beaten by a nose in the Suburban, was beaten a half length in a six-furlong sprint at Narragansett, then closed out the year with a win under 128 in the Whitney Trophy Handicap at Belmont.

After his three starts in 1935 at Santa Anita, Equipoise retired with a record of twenty-nine wins, ten seconds and four thirds and earnings of $338,610 in a career often interrupted by soundness problems. Had he been blessed with sound feet, one wonders just what his record may have been, but at any rate, he was one of the most beloved runners of his day.

DISCOVERY

With the retirement of Equipoise, racing fans were hungering for another hero that could carry heavy imposts and still defeat the best horses in training. In 1935, they found one in Alfred G. Vanderbilt's Discovery. In his final two seasons of racing, 1935 and 1936, Discovery stamped himself as one of the best weight carriers in decades.

It took him a while to get started as a two-year-old. Although owned by Vanderbilt, he raced for Adolph Pons that season, and it took him four starts to break his maiden. He won but twice. The year was 1933, and it was a filly year. He was out of the money in the Arlington Futurity won by the Dixiana filly Far Star. Colonel E.R. Bradley's fleet filly Bazaar beat him in the Hopeful, and Dixiana's champion filly Mata Hari bested him in both the Breeders' Futurity and Kentucky Jockey Club Stakes.

Discovery improved considerably at three, winning eight of his sixteen starts. He won the Brooklyn, the Kenner Stakes, the Whitney, the Rhode Island Handicap at Narragansett and the Potomac at Havre de Grace and closed the season with a win in the Maryland Handicap at Laurel. But Discovery had the misfortune of having been foaled the same year as Cavalcade, a colt by Lancegaye that went on to earn the three-year-old championship. They met six times, and Cavalcade won all six. Joe Estes, in a poem honoring Man 'o War titled "Big Red," perhaps gives the best description of Discovery's three-year-old season:

> *Young Equipoise had power*
> *to rouse the crowded stand,*
> *and there was magic in the name*
> *of Greentree's Twenty Grand,*
> *and Sarazen has sprinted,*
> *and Gallant Fox has stayed,*
> *and Discovery has glittered*
> *in the wake of Calvacade.*

With his three-year-old season behind him, Discovery launched into a string of thirty-three races spread over two years, 1935 and 1936, that stamped him as one of the all-time great weight carriers. He won the Merchants and Citizens Handicap under 139, the Brooklyn carrying 136, the Butler Handicap and the Arlington Handicap with 135 up. He won eight stakes carrying 130 or more plus the Whitney and the Wilson. His largest assignment came in the Merchants and Citizens Handicap in 1936 when he was asked to carry 143 pounds. He ran fifth, beaten six lengths with the first three carrying 100, 103 and 108. I checked out the chart of that one. It said that he tired. No kidding!

Discovery retired at age six to Vanderbilt's Sagamore Farm in Maryland. He ranked among the nation's leading sires five times, but it was as a broodmare sire that he excelled. Vanderbilt, when asked about his number-one theory in breeding runners, replied, "Breed a Discovery mare to anything." He had a point. A quick check showed that Bold Ruler, Native Dancer, Intentionally, Bed O' Roses, Hasty Road and Traffic Judge are among those produced by his daughters.

STAGEHAND

Stagehand was the champion three-year-old of 1938. Bred by Joseph E. Widener, he was by Sickle out of Stagecraft, by Fair Play. Fair Play, as you recall, sired Man 'o War. Stagehand was owned by Maxwell Howard and was trained by one of the all-time great jockeys, Earl Sande. In 1924, Sande was critically injured in a spill at Saratoga. At the time it was thought he was washed up as a jockey. But William Woodward coaxed him out of retirement and put him aboard Gallant Fox for the 1930 Kentucky Derby. As Gallant Fox came rolling home, famed writer Damon Runyon slipped a piece of paper into his typewriter and wrote:

> *Say have you turned the pages*
> *Back to the past once more?*
> *Back to the racing ages*
> *An a Derby out of the yore?*
> *Say, don't tell me I'm daffy,*
> *Ain't that the same ol' grin?*
> *Why it's that handy*
> *Guy named Sande*
> *…bootin' a winner in!*

Sande did a fine job training Stagehand as well. Stagehand's biggest win as a three-year-old came in the 1938 Santa Anita Handicap. He had won three in a row, the third being the Santa Anita Derby on February 22, 1938. That big win had come before the weights for the Santa Anita Handicap had been released, and Stagehand got in with an assignment of 100 pounds. He won by a nose, beating Seabiscuit under 130. Running third under 120 was the four-year-old Pompoon, a colt that had been the champion two-year-old in 1936.

After winning the Santa Anita Handicap, Stagehand headed to Churchill and ran third to The Chief and Lawrin in the Derby Trial. Lawrin went on to win the Kentucky Derby, and The Chief and Stagehand went to Aqueduct, where The Chief beat him two more times, first in the Dwyer then in the Brooklyn Handicap. Stagehand found the winner's circle in his next start, the Empire City Handicap, then ran fourth in the Arlington Classic and the Travers. Moving to Narragansett for his last three starts as a three-year-old, he was third, beaten by a neck in the J.C. Thornton Memorial, then beat Bull Lea in the Narragansett Special and Two Bob in the Governor's Handicap.

Stagehand began his four-year-old season with a win in the McLennan Memorial Handicap at Hialeah, at the expense of Bull Lea. Then, in what was to be his last start, Stagehand was third in the Widener Handicap won by Bull Lea. Retired to stud, he sired but three stakes winners.

Getting back to Pompoon, he was a consensus champion two-year-old in 1936 after winning six of his eight starts. He beat War Admiral down the straightaway Widener Course in the National Stallion Stakes, won the Jr. Champion Stakes and the Futurity and was a closing second to Whirlaway's half brother Reaping Reward in the New England Futurity.

Pompoon started his three-year-old season with a win in the Paumonok, ran fifth in the Wood Memorial, then went to Churchill for the Kentucky Derby to finish second to War Admiral, beaten by a length and a half. The Preakness was another matter. War Admiral and Pompoon were locked together the length of the stretch, with War Admiral prevailing by a head. I first heard about this race from Will Harbut, Man o' War's famous groom, at Faraway Farm. Often, if the listener wanted to hear more about Man o' War or one of his sons or daughters, Mr. Harbut would throw in a line about the 1937 Preakness, "and War Admiral looked over at Pompoon and said, 'Pompoon, my daddy broke John P. Grier's heart, come on!'" It made no difference to Mr. Harbut that John P. Grier went on to win several major stakes after that historic Dwyer. It was a great line! It gave me goosebumps every time I heard it.

War Admiral beat Pompoon by eighteen lengths in the Belmont of 1937. Pompoon went on at four to win several stakes. He was trained in his four-year-old season by John Loftus, who had been Man o' War's jockey his entire two-year-old season. For some reason, the powers that be refused to grant Loftus a jockey license for the next year despite Samuel Riddles's plea. But he went on to become a successful trainer. Pompoon won the San Carlos Handicap before running third in Stagehand's Santa Anita Handicap, then came back to win the Dixie Handicap at Pimlico and finish second in the Suburban, beaten by a nose by Snark while giving him nine pounds. At four in 1939, he started six times, with his best showings coming in his last two starts, seconds in the Massachusetts Handicap to Fighting Fox and Wilson Stakes at Saratoga to the high-class Eight Thirty. It's my recollection that Pompoon died before entering stud.

MENOW

Walk into the office at Mill Ridge Farm and one of the first things you see is a picture of Menow, a foal of 1935 by Pharamond II out of the 1930 Kentucky Oaks winner Alcibiades, by Supremus. This was pure Hal Price Headley breeding. He had imported Pharamond II, bred Alcibiades and stood Supremus at his Beaumont Farm. Mill Ridge is owned by Mr. Headley's daughter, Alice Chandler. Alice is a delight. I was visiting one day and happened to ask her about a colt named Whopper, bred by her father. "Oh yes," she said. "He died with his head in my lap." How's that for a tearjerker?

Alice is married to Dr. John Chandler, who came to this country from South Africa to join the veterinary firm of Hagyard, Davidson, and McGee. Back in the sixties, I bought a yearling by Kentucky Pride out of Mono, by Better Self from the Keeneland fall sales. Paid $3,000 for him, which happened to be my limit. He was a gelding, but that didn't bother me. He was bred by Howard Rouse, the manager of King Ranch, and I knew that he gelded all his colts as weanlings. I like to watch anything that interests me at the barn prior to the sale, looking for bad habits, even though I knew that Sam Hildreth once stated that he had turned down Man o' War because he was tearing the hell out of his stall. Dr. Chandler happened to be close by, so I asked him to look the gelding over. He did so, then came back and said he looked okay to him.

I named the gelding Wildcat Country, a name I picked up from a bumper sticker. After all, this was Lexington, home of the Kentucky Wildcats. Sold him to Tommy Heard, who took him to New York as a two-year-old, put him in at $20,000 claiming race and bet his money. He paid $9.20, was claimed and never started for claiming tag again, earning $144,000. For decades now, Dr. Chandler has been teasing me about how he had picked Wildcat Country out of the sale for me.

Getting back to Menow, he was the champion two-year-old in 1937 with an assignment of 126 pounds on the Experimental Free Handicap, 2 pounds above Tiger, a colt by Bull Dog bred by E.E. Shaffer. Tiger had a temperament that lived up to his name. He was scary mean as a stallion. Stood at E.K. Thomas's Timberlawn Farm in Bourbon County. Ranked at 121 pounds was Bull Lea, also bred by Shaffer, and he, as Tiger, was by Bull Dog.

Menow began his racing career in Chicago, breaking his maiden at Washington Park in his second start for trainer Duval Headley, then ran second to Tiger in the Washington Park Futurity. Menow was out of the money in the Arlington Futurity. But moving to New York he won the Champagne Stakes over Bull Lea and Fighting Fox, the latter a colt by Sir Galahad III bred by William Woodward Sr. In the Futurity, Menow beat Tiger and Fighting Fox.

The next year Menow was beaten by a neck by Bull Lea in the Blue Grass Stakes and was a pacesetting fourth in Lawrin's Kentucky Derby. Third in the Preakness, Menow then won the Withers and moved to the Massachusetts Handicap, beating War Admiral by eight panels of fence. War Admiral, then a four-year-old, was to lose but one more race that year, and that was his match race with Seabiscuit. Menow carried 107 pounds in the Massachusetts Handicap, War Admiral 130. Menow was to win one more stakes that year, the Potomac Handicap at Havre de Grace, beating Bull Lea.

Retired to Beaumont, Menow was a very successful sire. His best colts were Tom Fool and Capot. Tom Fool was bred by Duval Heatley and ran for Greentree Stable, and Capot was bred and raced by Greentree. Both were trained by John Gaver. In 1953, Tom Fool was undefeated in ten starts as a four-year-old to win Horse of the Year honors, outpolling Alfred Vanderbilt's three-year-old Native Dancer, whose only defeat had been that neck to Dark Star in the Kentucky Derby. Years later, in a discussion about the definition of what makes a great racehorse, Gaver was asked if Tom Fool was great. He thought it over for a while, then said, "Don't know about that, but he was damn good." Tom Fool became an outstanding sire even though he was noted for being slow covering his mares, a tendency he passed on to his sons. I remember being in line with a mare waiting our turn to be bred at Spendthrift Farm, and if Jester, a son of Tom Fool, was in front of you, you were in for a long wait.

Capot was Horse of the Year in 1949 after winning, among other stakes, the Preakness and the Belmont. He finished second to Calumet's Ponder in the Kentucky Derby. Capot was out of a daughter of St. Germans, a stallion with fertility problems that he passed on to several of his sons and grandsons, notably Triple Crown winner Assault and Kentucky Derby winner Middleground. As I recall, Capot turned out to be virtually sterile. That leads to the suspicion that infertility can also be passed on through the mare as well.

Menow also sired the champion filly Askmenow, a foal of 1940 out of Conclave, by Friar Rock, also bred by Hal Price Headley. She won the Selima Stakes at Laurel, but what likely earned the title was her performance in the Futurity, in which she ran second to Occupation with future Triple Crown winner Count Fleet third. The next year, she defeated colts to win the American Derby at Arlington Park. In 1946, Menow died at the age of eleven at Beaumont.

EL CHICO

El Chico was the two-year-old champion of 1938. He went to the post seven times, won seven times, all seven in stakes. Can't improve on that. He broke his maiden in the Youthful Stakes at Jamaica by four, going away. It was six weeks until his second start in the Dover Stakes at Delaware, and he won by a length. Moving to Aqueduct, he beat Lovely Night by four lengths in the Great American Stakes. His next three starts were at Saratoga. He won the United States Hotel Stakes in an eight-lengths romp over Invader and Eight Thirty. He next captured the Saratoga Special by three lengths, beating Eight Thirty and Third Degree, then won the Hopeful Stakes by two lengths over Ariel Toy and the next year's Kentucky Derby winner, Johnstown. His final start of the season resulted in a one-length win over Volitant and Johnstown in the Junior Champion Stakes at Aqueduct. El Chico was assigned top weight of 126 pounds on the Experimental Handicap, two more than Eight Thirty and Johnstown. Challedon, who would become the champion three-year-old of 1939, was assigned 122 pounds along with Porter's Mite and Xalapa Clown.

El Chico lost his first race in his first start as a three-year-old on April 15, 1939, going six furlongs in an allowance race at Jamaica. He broke alertly and went to the front, setting the pace, only to be nipped at the wire, losing by a nose to Gilded Night, a colt by Sir Galahad III bred by Wheatley Stable. Next time out was the Wood Memorial, and after a rough trip, he finished sixth, beaten fifteen lengths by Johnstown.

A week later, he forced the early pace in Johnstown's Kentucky Derby only to fade and beat two horses. The chart of the race noted that he "quit." That may have been a bit harsh. El Chico, I am told, means the "little one," and he indeed was small, basically a sprinter, and speed was his forte. Maybe the guy making charts that day at Churchill was having a hard time cashing tickets.

Moving to New York, El Chico ran a pacesetting second in an allowance race at Belmont, then posted back-to-back wins in allowance races at

Saratoga. The first was at a mile, and that was his only career win beyond six furlongs. He beat Third Degree going six furlongs in the second, and those were his only wins as a three-year-old. To be kind, it should be noted that he was five for five at Saratoga.

Next, El Chico was beaten by a nose by Olney, a colt by Burgoo King, in the Narragansett Handicap. He was to start four more times with his best showing a third in the Potomac Handicap at Havre de Grace. He was trained throughout his career by Matt Brady and ridden by Nick Wall in seventeen of his eighteen starts.

Many remember El Chico as a flash in the pan. Maybe so, but in my book, it was a damned bright flash. Any horse that could win seven stakes in a row would be welcome under my shed row. He was not the first, nor will he be the last, to be a disappointment as a three-year-old.

It should also be pointed out that El Chico was a member of a very good crop of runners. Johnstown, a son of Jamestown, became the first Kentucky Derby winner bred by A.B. Hancock Sr. He bred another when Jet Pilot won in 1947. Johnstown also won the Belmont Stakes by five lengths, the Withers and the Dwyer, and had he not developed a breathing problem no telling how good he would have been. Challedon, perhaps the best colt ever bred in Maryland, went on to be named champion three-year-old colt and Horse of the Year. Eight Thirty, a son of Pilate bred by George D. Widener, ranked near the top of his class again in 1939. Joe Palmer, in *A Quarter Century of American Racing*, listed only Johnstown and Challedon above him. John Hay Whitney's Porter's Mite also was no slouch. After winning a minor stakes at Tanforan in California and another at Detroit, he went to Belmont in the fall and set a new world record for six and a half furlongs in the Champagne Stakes and closed out his juvenile season with a win in the Futurity. Porter's Mite was by The Porter.

El Chico was bred by Leslie Combs, trustee, and sold to William Zeigler Jr. at Saratoga. El Chico was by John P. Grier out of La Chica, an unraced daughter of Sweep. He was the third foal out of La Chica. The first was stakes winner Planetoid, by Ariel. Planetoid was the dam of Grey Flight, winner of the Autumn Day Stakes and one of the all-time great producers. Grey Flight was the dam of nine stakes winners. In order, they were Full Flight, winner of five stakes; champion Misty Morn, by Princequillo; Gray Phantom; Misty Flight; Misty Day; Bold Princess; Bold Queen; Signore; and What a Pleasure. La Chica's second foal was Miyako, a full sister to El Chico. Miyako was the dam of steeplechase winner Columbus and also of the winner Geisha, dam of the great

Native Dancer. Next came El Chico, and he was followed by the quick Chicquelo, a colt by Ariel that won the Tremont Stakes.

On December 1, 1939, at Santa Anita, El Chico pulled up after a three-furlong workout with a fractured sesamoid of his left front and x-rays showed there was no possibility of saving him.

PAVOT

In 1941, Walter Jeffords took four Man o' War fillies out of training and sent them to be bred to Case Ace, standing nearby at Joseph Roebling's farm in New Jersey. Case Ace had good credentials. He was by Teddy and had won the Arlington Futurity at two and the Illinois Derby the following year. He was none too sound, however, and was soon retired to Roebling's farm. One of the Man o' War fillies was the winner Furlough, and the result of that mating was Ace Card. Ace Card won the Schuylerville, Polly Droumond and Gazelle, and she was later to produce four stakes winners for Jeffords: Post Card, Yildiz, My Card and One Count, a foal of 1949 by Count Fleet that was voted Horse of the Year in 1952. The other Man o' War filly was Coquelicot, also a winner, and in 1942 she produced a brown colt to be named Pavot. Pavot was the undefeated two-year-old champion of 1944. Coquelicot, I am told, is a flaming-orange variation from the Poppy family.

Pavot made his first start at Delaware and won by eight. He followed that with wins in the Christiana, the Mayflower, United States Hotel Stakes, the Hopeful and the Futurity. Only in the Hopeful was he tested, winning by a half length over Esteem, a colt by Stimulus out of champion Esposa that had won the Wakefield Stakes. At season's end Pavot was assigned co-highweight on the Experimental Handicap, sharing that honor with Free For All, a colt by Questionnaire that was undefeated in five outings, all in Chicago, with wins in the Arlington Futurity, Washington Park Futurity and the Hyde Park Stakes. John B. Campbell had assigned both colts 126 pounds, 3 more than yet another undefeated colt, C.V. Whitney's Burg-El-Arab, by Boojum, winner of the Tremont Stakes.

All three colts were disappointments at three. Free For All won but one more race, no stakes. Burg-El-Arab never raced again. Pavot went one for nine though his lone win was a big one. He won the Belmont Stakes by five lengths over Wildlife and Jeep. He also placed in four stakes.

Pavot did better at four, winning five of his fourteen starts including four stakes: the Sussex Handicap, Massachusetts Handicap, Wilson Stakes and, in what many consider to be the best performance of his career, a five-length win over Stymie and Rico Monte in the two-mile Jockey Club Gold Cup.

Pavot made two starts as a five-year-old to no avail and was retired to stud at Faraway, where he did moderately well siring twenty stakes winners. He died in 1968 at age twenty-six.

Burg-El-Arab, if memory serves, had fertility problems, but Free For All was another matter. He was the sire of Rough 'n' Tumble, probably the most influential sire ever to stand in Florida. Rough 'n' Tumble was the sire of one of the all-time greats, Dr. Fager, and the broodmare sire of the top sire In Reality.

A foal of 1948 out of the Bull Dog mare Roused, Rough 'n' Tumble won the 1951 Santa Anita Derby and the 1950 Primer Stakes with placings in the Garden State, Remsen, Futurity, Sheridan and San Felipe. He was bred by Dr. Charles Hagyard of the famed veterinary firm of Hagyard, Davidson and McGee. Dr. Hagyard had Free For All at stud on his farm just north of Lexington on Paris Pike, and the tough old stayer Stymie was also based there.

Rough 'n' Tumble sired twenty-three stakes winners. By many lengths, the best of them was Dr. Fager. In 1968 he was named Horse of the Year, champion handicap horse, champion sprinter and co-champion grass horse. He was a great weight carrier setting a world record for a mile, 1:32 and 1/5 under 132 pounds, and a new track record at Aqueduct under 139. Trainer John Nerud thought that Dr. Fager had a chance to break a record every time he went out. Dr. Fager was named after neurosurgeon Dr. Charles Fager, who saved Nerud's life after he was thrown from a pony and suffered a blood clot on the brain. Highly successful at stud Dr. Fager sired thirty-five stakes winners and died at age twelve in 1976.

BY JIMMINY

By Jimminy was the champion three-year-old of 1944. A bay, with no markings, he was by Pharamond II out of Buginarug, by Blue Larkspur, and he was bred by E.R. Bradley and raised on his Idle Hour Farm. He had been a good if not spectacular two-year-old, winning two times and finishing in the money eight times. His lone stakes win came in the Grand Union Hotel

Stakes at Saratoga beating Boy Knight with placings in the Pimlico Futurity, Albany Handicap, Hopeful Stakes and Richard Johnson Stakes. At year's end he was assigned 119 pounds on the Experimental Free Handicap. The 126 highweight was assigned to Pukka Gin, a Whitney colt by Firethorn. Then came Platter 124, Occupy 121 and Lucky Draw 120. Of these, Lucky Draw, a gelding by Jack High bred by George D. Widener, ended as the most successful. Racing to the age of seven he won sixteen times, including thirteen stakes, among them the Tremont, Youthful, Wood Memorial and the Peter Pan. He set a track record at Jamaica for a mile and a sixteenth, a track record at Monmouth, a mile and a quarter in 2:01 and 4/5, and equaled the world record for a mile and three-sixteenth at Narragansett, 1:54 and 3/5. He was one tough old warrior.

In 1943, after his win in the Grand Union Hotel, By Jimminy was sold to Alfred P. Parker for a price reported to be $20,000. He had been trained by J.W. "Jimmy" Smith, and while he continued his career in the Parker silks, he stayed with the Bradley Stable and Smith continued to train him.

By Jimminy was voted champion three-year-old colt almost by default. He began the season by finishing fifth against older horses in the Phoenix Handicap run that year at Churchill, winning his next start at Belmont, then running second to Who Goes There in the Withers, fourth in an overnight handicap, then beat Lucky Draw in yet another overnight handicap. By this time, Pensive had lost the form that he demonstrated by winning the 1944 Kentucky Derby. By Jimminy then won the Shevlin and the Dwyer, beating Stir Up, and then ran third to Stir Up and Lucky Draw in the Empire City Stakes. Stir Up was laid up, as was Who Goes There. So By Jimminy, with his three best rivals out of it, prevailed in his last three starts by winning the Travers, the American Derby and the Lawrence Realization. He was voted champion three-year-old colt. What have you done for me lately? Actually, the best three-year-old in 1944 was Calumet's brilliant filly Twilight Tear. She had rolled through the season, winning fourteen of her seventeen starts. At one time, she had won eleven in a row, and in her final start of the year, she beat the likes of Devil Diver in the Pimlico Special. Retired to stud in Virginia By Jimminy did not do well, as he was unpopular with breeders.

By Jimminy was not the first by Pharamond II to be named best of his division. In 1937, Menow, bred and owned by Hal Price Headley, was assigned 126 pounds on the Experimental. Fifth on the list that year was Bull Lea and both went on to become outstanding sires. Pharamond II was a full brother to the top sire Sickle, by Phalaris, out of Selene. Both were bred by

Lord Derby and Sickle was the better runner of the two. Pharamond II won the Middle Park Stakes at Newmarket at two and the Ellsmere Stakes at three was his lone win from eleven starts. He was offered for sale, the asking price $50,000. Hal Price Headley, owner of Beaumont Farm near Lexington, went to take a look. The story goes that it was practically dark when he arrived, it was a gloomy day and Pharamond II was barely discernible standing in his stall with straw nearly up to his knees. Headley didn't ask the groom to take the horse out of the stall, saying later, "I did not want Lord Derby's men to learn how interested I was." After returning to Kentucky, he wrote, "If Lord Derby would not be insulted I would like to offer 4,000 pounds [about $10,000] for Pharamond II." He got his horse.

BLUE PETER

One of the best sons of War Admiral was the ill-fated Blue Peter, a bay foaled in 1946 out of Carillion, by Case Ace, bred and owned by Joseph M. Roebling, owner of Harmony Hollow Stud in New Jersey. Andy Shuttinger had bred, raised and trained Feathers, the dam of Carillion, a daughter of Sun Briar. He sold her to Roebling but later trained Carillion and Blue Peter. Case Ace, by Teddy, was standing at the Roebling Farm.

Roebling had sent Carillion to Kentucky to be bred to War Admiral in 1945, and he decided to send her back in 1946 to be bred to War Relic. Blue Peter was foaled at Claiborne Farm in Kentucky.

Blue Peter ran third in a maiden special in April 1946 then broke his maiden in his second outing at the same track. Sent to Jamaica for the Youthful Stakes, he ran third to Eternal World and Arise but that was the last time he was to taste defeat. He won three straight at Garden State: an allowance race, the William Penn Stakes and the Garden State Stakes. Moving to Monmouth Park he won the Sapling then won two in a row at Saratoga—the Special and the Hopeful—and concluded his two-year-old season with a win in the Futurity at Belmont over the speedy filly Myrtle Charm, a daughter of Alsab. He ended the year with eight wins and two thirds in ten starts and with earnings of $189,185. In the history of racing only Occupation had earned more as a two-year-old with winnings of $192,355. Blue Peter was assigned 126 pounds on the Experimental Free Handicap, 2 more than Mr. Busher, another colt by War Admiral, 4 more than Capot and 5 more than Ocean Drive.

Shuttinger took Blue Peter to Aiken, South Carolina, for the winter and on June 18, 1949, it was reported that the colt was out for the year with a stomach ailment. Blue Peter died on January 12, 1950, because of an unknown ailment and was buried in the centerfield of the training track at Aiken. He was four years old.

I guess it's safe to say that Blue Peter was the best two-year-old colt sired by War Admiral. Ranked second to him on the Experimental was another son of War Admiral, Mr. Busher, a chestnut colt bred by Colonel E.R. Bradley's Idle Hour Stock Farm and owned by Maine Chance Farm. Mr. Busher was a full brother to the great Busher, Horse of the Year in 1945 after being voted champion two-year-old filly the previous year. Colonel Bradley died in 1946, and his entire Thoroughbred holdings were sold to a syndicate formed by Ogden Phipps, King Ranch and Greentree Stable. But before the split was accomplished the syndicate sold Busher's little brother Mr. Busher to Elizabeth Graham for $50,000, the highest price that had ever been paid for a weanling, and he competed in her Maine Chance silks. Mr. Busher started four times as a two-year-old and he won his first three including the National Stallion Stakes and the Arlington Futurity. He was injured in his fourth start, the Washington Park Futurity, and never raced again. Retired to stud he sired sixteen stakes winners and was the broodmare sire of thirty-two stakes winners, including White Star Line, a Northern Dancer filly who won the 1978 Grade 1 Kentucky Oaks and Grade 1 Alabama Stakes.

War Admiral topped the sire list in 1945, largely because of Busher's earnings, and ranked among the leading sires five times. A glance at his stud record leads you to believe that his best runners had been distaffers with a list headed by Busher. In *Thoroughbred Champions: Top 100 Racehorses of the 20th Century*, published by the *Blood-Horse*, she ranked fortieth, with only one distaffer ranked higher, the great Ruffian. Busher certainly dominated racing in 1945. Racing for Colonel Bradley, she won five of her seven starts at two and was named champion two-year-old filly in 1944. In March 1945, Bradley sold Busher to Louis B. Mayer for $50,000, and running for Mayer, she ran thirteen times at three, winning ten with two seconds and a third. She ran against her elders, she ran against the boys and even won a match race with Durazna, a four-year-old filly that had been champion at two. In what was perhaps her greatest race, she took on Calumet's tough handicapper Armed, gave him four pounds and beat him in the Washington Park Handicap, setting a new track record for ten furlongs in the process.

Busher did not start at four and made but one start at five and was unplaced. She was sold as a part of a dispersal for $135,000 to Neil McCarthy, then resold by McCarthy to Mrs. Graham for $150,000. She produced the excellent stakes winner Jet Action, a colt by Graham's 1947 Kentucky Derby winner Jet Pilot. Busher died at age thirteen from complications foaling.

Other top fillies by War Admiral were champions Searching; classic winner Busanda, winner of the Alabama and the Suburban and later the dam of the great Buckpasser; and Baba Kenny, who whipped the colts in the Hopeful. War Admiral was broodmare sire of 113 stakes winners, twice was the nation's leading broodmare sire and ranked among the leaders 14 times. Besides Buckpasser, his daughters produced champion Never Say Die, winner of the English Derby; champion Affectionately; champion Hoist the Flag; and champion Rose Jet.

DECATHLON AND WHITE SKIES

Two of the fastest sprinters of the twentieth century were White Skies and Decathlon. White Skies was a foal of 1948, a chestnut like his sire Sun Again, and his dam was Milk Dipper, by Milkman. Decathlon was foaled in 1953 by Olympia out of Dog Blessed, by Bull Dog. Both were foaled and raised on Hurstland Farm, which is on the outskirts of Midway, Kentucky, a small town halfway between Lexington and Frankfort, thus the name.

White Skies broke his maiden in his third try as a two-year-old and won his first stakes, the Princeton Handicap, in the fall at Garden State. He started seventeen times over the next two years, winning eleven, with two seconds and three thirds. His worst showing was a fourth under top weight of 128 pounds. Thereafter, he was never beaten by a horse that carried less weight. He picked up 130 to whip Hilarious (114) in the Sport Page Handicap. He won an overnight handicap at Gulfstream, giving the second horse 14 pounds. He won the Paumonok under 130 from Laffango (115). In the Toboggan, he ran six furlongs in 1:09 and 1/5 under 132 pounds, giving the second and third horses 24 and 10 pounds. Next came a win in the Roseben in which he ran seven furlongs in 1:22 and 2/5 under 132, giving the second horse 20 pounds. He was asked a bit too much in the Oceanport Handicap at Monmouth and ran second carrying 136 to Master Ace's 106. He went back to New York for his next effort and won the Carter Handicap under 133 over First Aid (115) and the tough South American–bred Royal Vale (126). In his next start he was beaten by a length while carrying 130 pounds by the classy Bobby Brocato (113), and in what proved to be the final start of his career, he ran third beaten by a neck for all the money, to Sailor (106) and Bobby Brocato (116) in the Toboggan at Belmont.

I was having trouble finding out what happened to White Skies, so I called a good friend of mine, Alfred Nuckols Jr. His dad was one of the Nuckols brothers who had operated Hurstland Farm for years. Alfred still lives in Midway, a lovely little town. The main street is Railroad Street, with train tracks right down the center, with shops and restaurants on each side. People who live in Midway never seem to leave, and those who want to live there better have a little money because housing is expensive. Alfred, of course, knew what had happened to White Skies. It seemed that shortly after the Toboggan, he broke down in a workout and couldn't be saved. Decathlon fared better.

It didn't take Decathlon long to find the winner's circle. He won his first five starts as a two-year-old in 1955. He was lucky to have made it to the races at all. He was sold by the Nuckols brothers to Robert J. Dienst, owner of Beulah Park and River Divide Farm, for $15,500, who turned him over to trainer Rollie Shepp. Shepp had Decathlon at Hialeah, and late in Decathlon's yearling year the horse stepped on a nail. The infection was so severe that it was weeks before Decathlon could put weight on it. A part of the foot was cut away, and when he did recover, it left him with an unusual gait. Jean Martin, who rode him in most of his races, said, "It feels like he's gonna fall apart under you."

Well, he may have moved funny, but he did it in a hurry. He won the Bay State Kindergarten Stakes at Suffolk Downs in his third start at two followed by a win in the Narragansett Stakes and the Tyro Stakes at Monmouth before losing his first race with a second in the Sapling, also at Monmouth. He was beaten that day by Needles, who won the 1956 Kentucky Derby and the three-year-old championship. Decathlon was to start seventeen times at two, adding two more stakes wins in December: the Desoto and Dade County Handicaps at Tropical Park.

In 1956, Decathlon posted twelve wins, five seconds and a pair of fourths. His stakes wins came in the Dade County Handicap and the Corals Gables Handicap at Tropical. In most of his wins, he sprinted six furlongs in 1:09 and change, and the handicappers had taken note of that. In his final start of the year, the Coral Gables, he was assigned 130 pounds, giving the second-place Flight Appeal 17 pounds and winning by three and a half lengths in 1:09 and 2/5.

Decathlon started nine times as a four-year-old and was asked to carry less than 130 pounds on only one occasion. He won the New Year's Handicap at

Tropical Park under 133 pounds, going six furlongs in 1:09 and 2/5, giving the second-place finisher 20 pounds. At Hialeah, he ran six furlongs in 1:09 and 2/5 to take the Hialeah Inaugural, carrying 135 to Best Appeal's 117.

Moving to Monmouth, he ran six furlongs in 1:08 and 2/5 to win the Oceanport Handicap, carrying 132 to beat Itobe (116). He came right back to take the Rumsen under 133, giving second-place Nahoodah 10 pounds. His lone defeat came in the Bristol Handicap at Narragansett. Under 134, he hit the rail on the turn and finished second. In his final three starts of the year, he sprinted seven furlongs in 1:21 and 3/5 to win the Longport Handicap at Atlantic City, giving Manteau 19 pounds; ran a dead heat with Lord Jeep (111) in the John Alden Handicap at Suffolk Downs under 133; and in the final start of his career, he carried 133 pounds and ran six furlongs in 1:09 and 3/5 to take the Princeton Handicap at Garden State.

At the end of his career Decathlon was retired for stud duties at Darby Dan. He was to sire twelve stakes winners, several that were best over a route of ground. Western Warrior won the United Nations Handicap, Juanita the Delaware Oaks and Doves Creek Lady the Suwannee Handicap. Eventually, Decathlon moved to Florida and died at nineteen in 1972.

According to Alfred, the Nuckols brothers commissioned a portrait of Milk Dipper, dam of White Skies, and Dog Blessed, dam of Decathlon, which hangs today in the farm office in Midway.

COALTOWN

I drove out to Keeneland to see the 1948 Blue Grass Stakes. I wanted to see Coaltown, the colt everybody was talking about, but I was rooting for Dixiana's Shy Guy. I wasn't 8 to 5 to make it. It was a pretty good drive from Dixiana to Keeneland, but "Maggy" my old 1935 Chevy got me there. I bought a Racing Form and took a look at the past performances. I knew that Shy Guy liked Keeneland. He had won the Breeders' Futurity the year before, so I was hoping for the best, thinking all this talk about Coaltown was because he belonged to Calumet and was trained by Ben Jones. Coaltown had not run at two; in fact, he nearly died. He had collapsed on the track while galloping and hemorrhaged from the head. When Jones rode up to him on his pony, he thought Coaltown was dying. "I wouldn't have given a quarter for him." Coaltown recovered but thereafter suffered from a mild breathing problem.

Coaltown made his first start as a three-year-old on February 3 at Hialeah going six furlongs and won by two and a half lengths. The chart said "won galloping." Three weeks later, he sprinted six furlongs in 1:09 and 3/5 and, as much the best, won by twelve. He was handled by Jimmy Jones in his first two outings, but he was sent to Keeneland for his third and then Ben took over, starting him against older horses in the six-furlong Phoenix Handicap, which he won by two and a half "ridden out."

By this time, Eddie Arcaro, who was scheduled to ride Coaltown's stablemate, Citation, in the Kentucky Derby, was having second thoughts. Back in 1942, John Gaver, trainer for Greentree Stable, had given Arcaro the choice of Devil Diver or Shut Out for the Derby. He picked Devil Diver. Shut Out won; Devil Diver finished sixth. So, when Arcaro asked Jones, the reply was, "Eddie, I wouldn't have put you on Citation if I didn't think he was the better horse."

I was having some doubts too, but mine didn't arrive until after the Blue Grass. Coaltown opened up six in the first quarter mile, led all the way and won by four and a half "eased up" over Billings, a colt by Mahmoud that went on to win several stakes in Chicago, notably the Hawthorne Gold Cup. Shy Guy ran third, trying as hard as he always did, but he was nowhere good enough. I came away convinced that I had seen in Coaltown the next Kentucky Derby winner. Arcaro went to Jones again. "Eddie," Jones said, "Citation can beat anything he can see, and there ain't nothing wrong with his eyes."

On Derby day, Citation proved that the senior Jones knew his horses. Coaltown led for the first mile, and then Citation kissed him goodbye and handily won by three and a half lengths with Arcaro aboard. N.L. Pierson, who had ridden Coaltown in the Blue Grass, was up again for the Derby and finished second, while Ben Whitaker's My Request was three lengths back of Coaltown, with Billings fourth.

Coaltown went on as a three-year-old to win the Swift, the Drexel at Washington Park and the Jerome, and he met Citation for the second time at Belmont on September 23 in the Sysonby. The result was the same. Citation won by three and a quarter with Coaltown third. They were separated by the fleet First Flight, a filly bred and owned by C.V. Whitney and a daughter of the Whitney stallion Mahmoud, winner of the 1933 English Derby. Mahmoud was a gray, and up until his progeny hit the tracks, there had been a general prejudice against gray horses. Dad sure didn't like them. Mahmoud changed all that—maybe not with Dad, but with most horsemen.

Coaltown came back at four to win twelve of his fifteen starts and was named champion handicap horse in 1949. Citation had gone out of training with ankles that persistently refused to stand hard training and was not to return until 1950. At the end of Coaltown's season, he held the world record for a mile, 1:34; had equaled the world record for a mile and a quarter at Gulfstream in 1:59 and 4/5; equaled Hialeah's six-furlong track record of 1:10 and 1/5; and equaled the mile and an eighth at Arlington Park in 1:48 and 2/5. The only two real blemishes on his records were handed him by Greentree Stable's Capot, a son of Menow trained by John Gaver. Capot had beaten him by a length in the Sysonby and by twelve lengths in the mile-and-a-sixteenth Pimlico Special. Those two defeats were Coaltown's last two starts of the year. He was to make eleven more starts over the next two years, winning but one, the Children's Hospital at Bay Meadows. In May of his six-year-old season Coaltown retired with a record of twenty-three wins, six seconds and three thirds from thirty-nine starts and earnings of $415,675.

Despite all he had accomplished there was some doubt among pundits about his courage. It was noted that he had neither won or lost a close one and had never, whether winner or loser, finished fighting powerfully with another horse. Looking back to his near death as a two-year-old in training and the fact that it left him with a breathing problem I consider that to be an unfair judgment. One thing is clear though, Coaltown was an absolute bust at stud.

Citation fared better at stud, though he never came close to siring anything near his ability. There is no disputing that he was a disappointment. Citation's best was the high-class filly Silver Spoon, the champion three-year-old filly of 1959. I saw her compete in Tomy Lee's Kentucky Derby, and she ran a credible fifth, beaten just three and a half lengths for all the money. She had run third to Sword Dancer and Easy Spur a week before the Derby, beaten two and a half lengths in a quick seven furlongs, 1:22 and 1/5. She had beaten colts in the Santa Anita Derby and had won her first six starts. Among those were the three filly stakes: La Centinela, Santa Ynez and Santa Susana, all three at Santa Anita. After the Derby, she went back to California and won the Cinema Handicap beating colts, then came back east to run second to Resaca in the Delaware Oaks, beat Indian Maid and Royal Native in an allowance race at Monmouth and finished third in the Monmouth Oaks to Royal Native and Indian Maid. Tough company! Silver Spoon ran fourteen times at four and won five stakes, all against her own sex. She turned in game runs against males several times with no wins and retired with a record of thirteen wins, three seconds and four thirds from twenty-seven starts.

Silver Spoon was bred and owned by C.V. Whitney and trained through most of her career by Bob Wheeler. Retired to the C.V. Whitney Farm she produced the good stakes winner Inca Queen, a filly by Hail To Reason that won the Demoiselle and the Columbiana, Top Flight and Sheepshead Bay Handicaps. Another daughter, the winner Silver Coin, by Never Bend, produced Florida Derby winner Coined Silver. Silver Spoon has one of those pedigrees that makes you think your computer is never going to stop printing.

Citation ended up siring but twelve stakes winners. Fabius won the Preakness, Beyond won the Acorn and Citation was just fifteen when he passed away at Calumet. No son of Bull Lea came close to emulating his sire at stud, and it's interesting that, though he topped the sire list five times, Bull Lea's stud career tailed off the last five or six years of his career.

Getting back to Silver Spoon, her dam was Silver Fog, a winning daughter of Mahmoud and dam also of stakes winners The Searcher, by the Whitney home stallion Phalanx, and Silver Bright by Barbizon, a son of Polynesian. Barbizon was champion two-year-old in the crop of 1954 that included the likes of Bold Ruler, Round Table and Gallant Man.

Mahmoud's lone win as a three-year-old came in the 1936 English Derby. He was sent to the yearling sale at Deauville with a reserve set at 5,000 guineas. Abe Hewitt, in his book *Sire Lines*, published in 1977 by the *Blood-Horse*, said that when the reserve price was not reached, Mahmoud was sent to trainer Frank Butters, who had charge of the Aga Khan's horses at Newmarket. On the day that Mahmoud arrived, Butters got a call from the Aga Khan.

"What do you think of the gray colt I sent you from France?"

"I think he's all right."

"What do you think he would bring at auction in England?"

"Around 8,000 guineas."

"Do you really? In that case I think I will keep him."

In 1940, C.V. Whitney bought Mahmoud for about $85,000 and brought him to Kentucky, where he became an immediate success, siring seventy stakes winners. Mahmoud died in 1962 at the age of twenty-nine and is buried on the property that is now Gainesway Farm.

SWEET PATOOTIE

Sweet Patootie was the champion two-year-old filly of 1952. Don't you just love that name? Sweet Patootie was bred by Coldstream Farm, owned by E.E. Dale Shaffer at the time, ran for Mrs. Shaffer and was trained by Howard Battle, who later was the longtime racing secretary at Keeneland. Nice guy. She was by Alquest, a son of Questionaire that stood at the farm owned by A.C. Ernst on the Old Frankfort Pike in Fayette County, and was out of Sweet Woman, by Roman.

Sweet Patootie started twelve times as a two-year-old and won eight with four seconds. She won first time out in March, going three furlongs in :34 flat at Gulfstream, then ran second in her next two starts. She won for the second time at Detroit, then tried her first stakes and ran second to Biddy Jane, another filly with a fun name, in the Miss America Stakes at Hawthorne. Biddy Jane was by Psychic Bid, and she could fly. She equaled the track record for three furlongs at Gulfstream, :32 and 4/5; set a new track record at Gulfstream, four and a quarter furlongs in :52 and 4/5; and equaled the five-furlong track record at Hawthorne of :59 flat.

In her last seven starts as a two-year-old, Sweet Patootie posted six wins and a second. She won at Detroit by four, at Atlantic City by five, beat colts in the Longport at Atlantic City by four, went to Narragansett and won the Jeanne d'Arc Stakes by seven, then under 127 pounds was beaten by a nose by Piedmont Lass in the Margate at Atlantic City. Sweet Patootie was giving Piedmont Lass 16 pounds. Ten days later, they met again in the Frizette at Jamaica at equal weights, and Sweet Patootie beat her by a length and a quarter. Piedmont Lass was by Thellusson, a son of Gallant Fox that nobody had ever heard of. On October 18, Sweet Patootie closed out her juvenile season with a win over Good Call and Aerolite in the Alcibiades Stakes at Keeneland. I was working for Uncle Sam at the time and unfortunately didn't get to see that one. She never won again. In nine starts as a three-year-old, she was in the money but once, finishing third to Cerise Reine and Bubbly in the Ashland Stakes at Keeneland after setting the early pace. Cerise Reine was by Requested, like Sweet Patootie's sire Alquest, a son of the Greentree stallion Questionaire. Cerise Reine won the Delaware Oaks and was second to Bubbly in the Kentucky Oaks. Bubbly, by Bull Lea, was one of five stakes winners out of Calumet's high-class stakes winner Blue Delight, by Blue Larkspur.

Sweet Patootie's dam, Sweet Woman, a daughter of the top-speed sire Roman, won four times and ran second in the Myrtlewood Stakes. Sweet

Woman produced twelve foals; all twelve got to the races, and eleven won. In addition to Sweet Patootie, Sweet Woman was the dam of Lady Swaps, winner of the Colonial and Regret Handicaps, and I'm For More, by another speed sire, Olympia. I'm For More won the Dover Stakes, set a new track record for five and a half furlongs at Monmouth and placed in the Tremont and National Stallion Stakes. He was a useful sire while standing in Florida. Sweet Woman's daughters became stakes producers, but Sweet Patootie was not one of them. She produced seven named foals by a variety of stallions, namely Citation, Counterpoint, Intent, Watch Your Step, two by King of the Tudors and Vertex, seven winners. All were colts.

BARBIZON

I guess it's safe to say that the best crop of foals ever to race in North America arrived in 1954. What a crop that was! Bold Ruler and Round Table arrived on the same night at Claiborne Farm. Gallant Man, bred by the Aga Khan and Prince Aly Khan, was foaled in Ireland. Gen. Duke was foaled at Calumet Farm, as was his stablemate Iron Liege. Then there was Vertex, Federal Hill and Clem, and there may have been one or two that have slipped my mind, but those will do.

When you throw in the fact that Bold Ruler, Round Table, Gallant Man and Vertex were highly successful at stud and that Clem also did very well, I stand firm that this was the best crop of all. There is one name that I didn't mention, and that was the champion two-year-old colt of 1956, Barbizon.

Barbizon, like Gen. Duke and Iron Liege, was bred by Calumet Farm. He was by Polynesian, winner of the Preakness and Champion Sprinter who stood at Ira Drymon's Gallaher Farm on the Russell Cave Pike near Lexington, and his dam was the fine race mare Good Blood, by Bull Lea. Good Blood won the Arlington Matron, the Princess Pat, the Vineland Handicap and the Queen Isabell Handicap, and she also produced Hillsborough, a colt by Calumet's 1949 Kentucky Derby winner Ponder. Hillsborough won a couple of stakes and ran second in the Jockey Club Gold Cup. Good Blood also was the ancestress of a whole passel of stakes winners.

Barbizon reeled off four straight wins to start his career, the first three at Belmont under Arcaro. Moving to Garden State, he won a one-mile allowance race under Bill (don't call me Willy!) Hartack then lost for the first time by three-fourths of a length by failing to catch the fleet Federal

Hill, a colt by Cosmic Bomb. That was a prep for the Garden State Stakes, at the time the richest race in the world for two-year-olds, where he was to meet Bold Ruler.

Bold Ruler went into the race off seven wins and a second in his first eight starts. He won the Youthful Stakes at Jamaica in his third start then the Juvenile at Belmont in his fifth. In his sixth, on a sloppy track down the Widener Chute at Belmont, he bore out and was beaten by Nashville, who, like Bold Ruler was a son of Nasrullah, then he bounced right back to beat the good colt Missile, by War Relic, down the same Widener Chute, getting the six furlongs in 1:08 and 3/5. Eight days later, on October 13, he came down the Widener Chute in 1:15 and 1/5 for the six and a half furlongs to win the Futurity by over two lengths from Greek Game and Amarullah.

Bold Ruler was the favorite to win the Garden State Stakes run on October 27. The track was labeled good. He stumbled early and was never in contention, finishing seventeenth of nineteen, beaten twenty-four lengths by Barbizon. His next start, ten days later, was in the Remsen at Jamaica. After a poor break he dropped out of it and was eased. Those two losses cost him the two-year-old championship, with the honor going to Barbizon.

Barbizon was a disappointment at three, winning but twice, an allowance race at Garden State and another allowance test later in the year also at Garden State. In his only stakes placing he was beaten by a nose by Jet Colonel in the Hutchinson at Gulfstream. Late in the season he was privately sold to Warner Jones Jr., owner of Hermitage Farm near Goshen, Kentucky. He ran twice for Jones at four with his best effort a fourth in the New Year's Handicap at Tropical Park and was retired to stud. His final line read twenty-one starts, seven wins and a pair of thirds for earnings of $199,400.

Barbizon sired forty-three stakes winners while standing at Hermitage, and Jones, who used to advertise his sale yearlings as "moneymakers," had a moneymaker in Barbizon. Many of his better stakes winners were fillies. Pam's Ego won the Frizette, the Barbara Fritchie, the Comely and the Mermaid. Silver Bright won the then important Arlington Washington Lassie, Dottie's Doll the Molly Pitcher and the Hempstead, Charspiv the Distaff and Rhubarb the Colleen. His daughters produced seventy-one stakes winners. Listed among the seventy-one were Beldale Ball, winner of the Melbourne Cup; Grade 1 winner Tsunami Slew; Grade 1 winner State Dinner; and Grade 1 winner Banquet Table. Barbizon died at age twenty-nine at Hermitage Farm.

One of my favorites from the class of '54 was Clem, so much that I went as far as to buy a yearling by him at a sale up East. Paid $2,000 for him, sold him for $10,000 and he won his first start as a two-year-old. Clem was one tough cookie. He took on all comers and won his share. Give him enough weight and he beat many of the best. Ask Round Table. Joe Estes, in the 1958 edition of *American Race Horses*, wrote, "Of the many horses which have been heralded as giant killers, few have proved more murderous than Clem was in 1958."

Clem was bred by Louis B. Mayer and sold to Adele Rand for $8,500 at the 1955 Keeneland Summer Sale. He was by the Australian champion Shannon II, who had been imported and was retired to stud at Leslie Combs's Spendthrift Farm. Clem was by many lengths his sire's best runner. Impulsive, Clem's dam, was by Supremus, and she also was the dam of the tough handicap horse Silverado, by Requested, and Canadian Oaks winner Miss Ardan, dam of Coaltown Cat.

Clem won the Absecon Island Stakes, ran second in the Sanford and Saratoga Special and took third in the World Playground Stakes as a two-year-old. He pulled off his first upset in the 1956 Arlington Classic by defeating Kentucky Derby winner Iron Liege. Less than a month later, he broke a pedal bone in his near fore hoof and was through for the year.

In 1958, Clem won the United Nations Handicap, setting a new track record, then set another track record to take the one-mile Washington Park Handicap in 1:34, lowering Equipoise's track record by two-fifths of a second. Round Table nosed out Nadir for second. Clem carried 110, Round Table 131. In the beaten field were the likes of Swoon's Son and Bardstown.

Clem, under 113, met Round Table, 130, next in the United Nations Handicap. Ridden by Bill Shoemaker, Clem led nearly all the way then held off Round Table by half length while taking a full second off the track record. Clem and Round Table met again, this time at level weights, in the Woodward. Shoemaker took Clem to the front again and Arcaro, on Round Table, kept him lapped on the smaller Clem for nearly three-quarters of a mile before dropping back. But Clem was not given the luxury of a breathing spell. Bill Boland, on the three-year-old Nadir, immediately moved up and for nearly five-sixteenths of a mile the two ran head to head. A lesser horse would have folded, but there was no quit in Clem. He held on to win by a half length. After the race Shoemaker said, "He's as game a horse as I ever rode."

Clem retired to stud after posting twelve wins, eight seconds and thirteen thirds against the best of his era for earnings of $535,681. In addition to the races mentioned, he won the Withers and the Palm Beach Handicap and sired eighteen stakes winners and a host of hard-hitting runners.

Bold Ruler was not only the best sire from the crop of 1954 but also the best of the twentieth century if you measure success by the number of times he ranked at the top of the sire list—eight times. Star Shoot ranked number one five times in the early part of the twentieth century, followed by Calumet Farm's Bull Lea with five and Nasrullah, sire of Bold Ruler, five. Round Table was the nation's leading sire in 1972. Gallant Man did not reach the pinnacle of success of either Bold Ruler or Round Table, but he was pretty darn good. He sired fifty-one stakes winners, among them champion filly Gallant Bloom for King Ranch, Coraggioso, the good sprinter and sire Gallant Romeo, and My Juliet, one of the fastest sprinters of either sex, who won twenty-four times including the Vosburgh. Spicy Living won the Mother Goose, My Gallant won the Blue Grass Stakes and Road Princess won the Mother Goose. Gallant Man's daughters produced eighty-nine stakes winners, including Kentucky Derby winner Genuine Risk and champion two-year-old Lord Avie.

Vertex was always one of my favorites. He developed a bit slower than his contemporaries in the foal crop of 1954, but at four and five he was the leading handicap horse in the East. That means he was the second best in the nation, as Round Table was a dominant force on the West Coast and in Chicago. Vertex was by the good sire The Rhymer, a son of St. Germans that stood up East. The Rhymer dodged the infertility problems that dogged many prominent sons of St. Germans, notably Assault and Twenty Grand. Daughters of St. Germans also passed on their infertility to their sons. Greentree's Horse of the Year, Capot, was out of a St. Germans mare, and I don't recall him siring a single foal.

Vertex had no problem. He was a grand-looking horse, a liver chestnut, and stood at Danada Farm on the Old Frankfort Pike. He was the sire of Lucky Debonair, winner of the 1965 Kentucky Derby by a neck over Dapper Dan and Tom Rolfe, a race I happened to see. Dapper Dan was one of those come-from-behind runners that was always closing but never got there. He also ran second in the Preakness to Tom Rolfe but never won a stakes. He was by Ribot and ended up in Japan.

Lucky Debonair went into the Derby off wins in the Santa Anita Derby and the Blue Grass Stakes and later sired Irish Derby winner Malacate and fourteen other stakes winners before going to Venezuela.

Vertex was the sire of champion two-year-old Top Knight, winner of the Champagne, the Futurity and the Hopeful Stakes and the following year, the Flamingo and the Florida Derby. Top Knight beat two real good horses in the Florida Derby: Arts and Letters and Al Hattab. He was the second choice to win it all in the 1969 Kentucky Derby but stopped badly after setting the early pace. The race was won by Majestic Prince after a bitter duel with Arts and Letters. Majestic Prince was a gorgeous colt, a real eye-catcher on the lines of Secretariat. I found out later that he was a cribber. I hate cribbers. That's like finding out that Mary Poppins was a junkie! Top Knight never won another race after the Florida Derby.

Majestic Prince went on to win the Preakness again at the expense of Arts and Letters but was beaten in the Belmont Stakes, a race in which he should have never started. He went into the Belmont over the objections of his trainer, John Longdon, but owner Frank McMahon insisted. We all make mistakes. Bred by Leslie Combs II, Majestic Prince went to stud at Combs's Spendthrift Farm, siring Belmont Stakes winner Coastal and Majestic Light. Among Majestic Light's better runners were Kentucky Oaks winner Lite Light and Wavering Monarch, sire of champion two-year-old Maria's Mon. Maria's Mon, retired to stud at Pin Oak Stud, sired the 2001 Kentucky Derby winner Monarchos and the 2010 Kentucky Derby winner Super Saver.

DARK MIRAGE

Dark Mirage was the champion three-year-old filly of 1968, and the book remains open as to just how good she was. She was bred by Duval Headley, raised at his Manchester Farm, and sold for $6,000 as a yearling to Lloyd Miller. She was very small, barely 15 hands. Her sire, Persian Road II, was standing at stud at Manchester, and we will also never know just how good he was. He was by Persian Gulf, a son of Bahram, and he had raced in England, where he won the Ebor Handicap, the Great Yorkshire Handicap and the Manchester Cup. He sired several nice stakes winners—Persian Intrigue and Dartsum come to mind—but he died the same year that his main claim to fame, Dark Mirage, was voted champion three-year-old filly.

It took Dark Mirage a while to get rolling. Not that it was for a lack of trying. She started seventeen times at two, winning two races. She broke her maiden in her fourth start, taking a maiden special at Saratoga, and came back ten days later to win an allowance race at the same track. She competed in five stakes at five different tracks, with her best efforts coming in the Goldenrod at Churchill, where she was fourth, and she was a close fifth in the Gardenia at Garden State.

Dark Mirage had the same connections as a three-year-old. She was owned by Lloyd Miller and trained by E.W. King, but she was a completely different filly. After running fourth in her first start of the year in an allowance race at Aqueduct, she reeled off nine straight wins. She won a one-mile allowance race at Aqueduct by nine lengths on March 2 under Ron Turcotte.

On April 3, she won Aqueduct's Prioress Stakes by a length with Angel Cordero aboard. For the balance of the season, her regular rider was Manuel Ycaza.

Moving on to Churchill Downs, Dark Mirage won the La Troienne by three lengths from the talented Lady Tramp, a daughter of imported Sensitivo.

Six days later she won the Kentucky Oaks by four and a half lengths besting Miss Ribot. On May 23, she won the Acorn Stakes at Belmont, getting the mile in 1:34 and 4/5, beating Another Nell and Lady Tramp. She won by six. She won the Mother Goose Stakes on June 10 by ten lengths over Guest Room and Parida.

Twelve days later, she won the Coaching Club American Oaks by twelve over Guest Room and Syrian Sea. Moving to New Jersey, Dark Mirage won the Monmouth Oaks by four from Singing Rain on the Fourth of July.

Her last start of the season was on July 27 in the Delaware Oaks. Actually, it was a betless exhibition run between the seventh and eighth races. She won by two lengths over three other fillies that were competing for place money. There was no question as to who was the champion three-year-old filly of 1968.

Dark Mirage continued her win streak with her first start at four, a win in the Santa Maria Handicap at Santa Anita. Ten in a row. On March 1, she went to the post for the Santa Margarita under 130 pounds with Eddie Belmonte up. The track was sloppy. Roughed at the start she ducked out on the first turn and broke down. Extended attempts to save her proved futile. At one time during her three-year-old season rival trainer Max Hirsch observed, "I'm not at all sure that little filly can't beat them all, Dr. Fager, Damascus, any of them, at a mile and a half, scale weights." What we should remember about Dark Mirage was that she was the first filly to sweep the Acorn, the Mother Goose and the Coaching Club American Oaks.

6

Should Have Been Champions

EIGHT THIRTY

George D. Widener's Eight Thirty was, in my opinion, one of the best racehorses never to be named champion. I'll admit to a certain bias here. I grew up looking at Eight Thirty when he was turned out on George Widener's Old Kenny Farm right next door to Dixiana. Not only that, he was one of the best-looking horses I've ever seen.

Eight Thirty was a chestnut foaled in 1936 by Pilate out of Dinner Time, by High Time. He won the Flash Stakes and the Christiana Stakes at two and ran second in the Futurity and the Saratoga Special and third in the United States Hotel Stakes. As a three-year-old, he won the Travers, the Whitney, the Wilson and Diamond State Stakes and the Saratoga Handicap. He won seven of his ten starts and earned just $39,125 for his efforts, which tells you something about purses at the time. It also was a good year for three-year-olds, with Challedon, Johnstown, Hash and other good ones.

Joe Palmer, in *A Quarter Century of American Racing*, listed only Challedon above Eight Thirty as a four-year-old, even though Eight Thirty beat Challedon in the Massachusetts Handicap. He also won the Suburban under 127 pounds, beating the handy Can't Wait (109); the Toboggan, carrying 127 sprinting six furlongs in 1:09 and 4/5; and the Wilson Stakes. Listed below him were the likes of Seabiscuit and Kayak II. Eight Thirty returned at five in 1941 to win the Metropolitan and the Toboggan again, came up with a bad ankle and retired with earnings of $155,475. In twenty-seven starts, he won sixteen races with three seconds and five thirds. He was unplaced but three times, never more than once in a single season.

Standing at Old Kenny Farm, Eight Thirty's record at stud was as good as his record at the races. He never topped the sire list, but he was knocking on the door several times. He sired forty-four stakes winners, and several of his sons did well at stud. His fleet Sailor was bred and owned by Brookmeade Stable and trained by Preston Burch. Sailor was a foal of 1952, and he was dead game and versatile, winning major sprints like the Toboggan and the Fall Highweight Handicap. He grabbed himself coming out of the gate for the 1955 Toboggan and won it anyway. Later, he defeated Nashua in the Gulfstream Park Handicap, getting the mile and a quarter in 2:00 and 2/5, and he was third—beaten by two noses—in the Widener Handicap to Nashua, who was making his first start as a four-year-old, and Alfred Vanderbilt's Social Outcast. Sailor injured his ankle shortly after winning the John B. Campbell Handicap as a four-year-old and was syndicated for stud duties at Darby Dan Farm, where he sired twenty stakes winners, among them champion Bowl of Flowers.

Another son of Eight Thirty to do well at stud was Bolero, standing at Lou Dougherty and Harold Snowden's Stallion Station on Russell Cave Pike in Lexington. Bolero had speed to burn! Racing on the West Coast, he set four new track records going six furlongs and a world record at seven furlongs at Santa Anita, 1:21 flat. He also won the nine-furlong Del Mar Derby. Bolero sired thirty-four stakes winners, among them the useful sire Our Michael, a horse I had some luck breeding to when he was standing at Henry White's Plum Lane Farm. Royal Coinage, winner of the Saratoga Special, Sapling and Great American Stakes as a two-year-old in 1954, also stood at the Stallion Station. He sired the 1960 Kentucky Derby winner Venetian Way and was the broodmare sire of the 1975 Preakness winner Master Derby.

But the two Eight Thirtys that I recall most were Here's Hoping and Lights Up. Here's Hoping was a black filly foaled in 1947 out of the handy race mare Saran, by St. Germans, bred by Mr. Fisher and raced in the Dixiana silks. Lights Up was a chestnut colt out of Tedmelia, by Teddy, bred and owned by George D. Widener.

Joe Palmer, in the 1949 edition of *American Race Horses*, described Here's Hoping as the best two-year-old in the West, meaning Chicago. She won the Princess Pat Stakes and the Tomboy Stakes and came back at three to win the Cleopatra and later the Churchill Downs Handicap. She loved Keeneland, setting a new track record for six and a half furlongs that lasted just the year because she came back and broke her own track record in 1952.

Lights Up broke his maiden in his eighth start as a two-year-old at Aqueduct, then won his last two, including the Remsen, and was assigned 114 on the Experimental Handicap. The next year he started by running third in the Everglades before winning on May 25 at Belmont. On June 3, 1950, he won the Peter Pan, beating Hal Price Headley's Mr. Trouble. He finished a strong second in the Belmont Stakes to King Ranch's Middleground, winner of the 1950 Kentucky Derby, third to Hill Prince and Greek Song in the Dwyer and moved to Monmouth to win the Lamplighter Handicap over Ferd and Post Card. After running second to Sunglow (later the sire of Sword Dancer when he stood at Mereworth Farm) and second by a nose to Greek Ship in the Choice Stakes, Lights Up hit a home run by winning the Travers over Alfred Vanderbilt's talented filly Bed O' Roses, by Rosemont.

I crossed paths with Lights Up in the summer of 1952 at Golden Gate Fields in California. The track is located on San Francisco Bay, where I had been sent to a school right out of boot camp. I had a ball that summer. Learned to love Dixieland music by listening to Bob Scobey, Turk Murphy and Clancy Hayes, who, incidentally, attended Centre College in Danville, Kentucky. Of course, this was back when you could walk down the street in San Francisco without stepping in something.

Anyway, Dad had wrangled a clubhouse pass to Golden Gate. I went every chance I could and one day there was Lights Up in a feature race. The favorite that day was a horse named Phil D. and I got something like 9–2 on Lights Up and he won. The next Saturday the two met again and Phil D. was again the favorite. Lights Up was 3–1, and he won again. Here I am, going on seven decades later, and I still remember Lights Up.

Getting back to Eight Thirty, his dam, the High Time mare Dinner Time, also was the dam of the filly named Time To Dine, by Jamestown. She won at three and later produced the talented filly Seven Thirty, by Mr. Music, an unraced full brother to Spy Song. Bred by Mr. Widener, Seven Thirty won the Comely, Delaware Handicap, Black Helen Handicap and Bed O' Roses Handicap and placed in six more stakes, among them the Acorn, for earnings of $234,956. She was a foal of 1958 and her first foal, a colt by Bold Ruler, arrived in 1964. That was the high-class Bold Hour, winner of the Futurity, Hopeful and Flash Stakes at two and later the Amory L. Haskell, Grey Lag, Saranac, Benjamin Franklin Handicap and the Discovery. Quite a family there, all started by a High Time mare.

SWOON'S SON

We talk about Eight Thirty being one of the best racehorses never to be voted champion. Another is E. Gay Drake's Swoon's Son. A foal of 1953, Swoon's Son was by The Doge out of Swoon, by Sweep Like, owned, bred and raised on Drake's Mineola Farm just north of Lexington on Bryan Station Pike. Swoon's Son won stakes at two, three, four and five but it was his three-year-old season when he should have been named champion. Instead, honors went to Needles, winner that year of the Kentucky Derby, the Belmont and the Florida Derby. I am not alone in my opinion. The following is from *American Race Horses, 1956*:

> *At the end of 1956 Swoon's Son got only a scattering of votes for best three-year-old, but the majority of opinion was suspect. The year's end honors went to Needles, a very good colt, but this was only because of the great American game of over simplification. There was nothing in the books to suggest that Needles was as good as Swoon's Son at distances up to a mile and an eighth. There was no convincing evidence that he was superior to Swoon's Son at any distance. If one falls into the evil habit of reflection upon such matter, there arises the doleful speculation that the honors go to the horse with the most publicity. No other 3 year old in North America was as fast, consistent, or as versatile as Swoon's Son.*

Needles was the first Florida-bred colt to win the Kentucky Derby, and he put Ocala on the map. I recall an article in *Sports Illustrated* singing the praises of Florida as the ideal place to raise Thoroughbreds and asserting that the Ocala area would soon equal the Blue Grass of Kentucky. Didn't happen. They raise very good horses in Florida, but they are still number two.

Swoon's Son, in twelve starts as a three-year-old, won ten and was twice second. He won the American Derby, Arlington Classic, Chicagoan Stakes, Clark Handicap, Warren Wright Memorial and the Domino Stakes. After Swoon's Son's score in the American Derby his rider, Dave Erb, said, "This is the best three-year-old I have ever ridden." Erb had ridden Needles to win the Kentucky Derby and Belmont Stakes. Add his name to the list of believers in Swoon's Son. At the end of his career Swoon's Son had won thirty times, on dirt and grass; set or equaled track records at Keeneland, Washington Park, Arlington and Hawthorne; and earned $970,605.

Few breeders or owners have gone through better years of racing than Mr. Drake experienced from 1954 through 1958. Dogoon, a full brother to Swoon's Son, was a year his senior, and he, too, was a high-class stakes winner. He had started the ball rolling by winning the Hawthorne Juvenile Stakes as a two-year-old, and by career's end Dogoon had won twenty-eight races and six stakes and had set or equaled track records at Keeneland, Detroit, Washington Park, Churchill Downs and Hawthorne. Add it up. Between the two brothers, they won fifty-eight races and earned $1,190,965.

I recall seeing both Swoon's Son and Dogoon at Keeneland. Mr. Drake would bring them in around the beginning of February, get them ready for spring racing at Keeneland or Churchill Downs, take them to Chicago for the summer, bring them back for fall racing in Kentucky and turn them out for the winter. No year-round racing. Perfect.

Retired to stud at Drake's Mineola Farm, Swoon's Son did very well, although he never received the backing given lesser runners with more popular pedigrees. His sire, The Doge, by Bull Dog, had been useful, but Swoon's Son was by many lengths his best. Swoon's Son sired twenty-two stakes winners, among them Chris Evert, winner in 1973 of the Coaching Club American Oaks, Mother Goose and Acorn. He also was the broodmare sire of Bag of Tunes, winner that same year of the Kentucky Oaks. Swoon's Son died at Mineola in 1977.

7

Three Derbys

HOOP JR.

The first Kentucky Derby winner that I actually picked through handicapping was Hoop Jr. in 1945. Dad had arranged to have the *Daily Racing Form* delivered to the farm, and he would bring it home. This grabbed my attention, and I would begin to pick up copies of various sports magazines that carried betting systems in Lexington at the Fayette Cigar Store on Main Street. It's still there, only moved a couple of blocks east across from where the Phoenix Hotel used to be. The *Turf and Sport Digest* was my favorite magazine, excluding the *Blood-Horse*.

In 1945 the Derby was run on June 9 because of a wartime ban on racing lasting four months, before ending on V-E Day, May 8, 1945.

There was a field of sixteen for the 1945 Derby, and the slight favorite was Calumet Farm's Pot O' Luck. Hoop Jr. was the second choice and I liked him because he had won the Wood Memorial and seemed to be peaking. The track came up muddy and Hoop Jr. had shown a liking for an off track as a two-year-old. Although he had never won a stakes, he placed in three for trainer Ivan Parke. The last race of his two-year-old season came on June 13 at Suffolk Downs, which Hoop Jr. won, beating his stablemate, but he came out of the race with ankle problems. His owner, Fred W. Hooper, said facetiously, "Let's put this colt away and win the Kentucky Derby with him." Less then a year later, after finishing with the Derby Cup presentation and walking back to the stable to watch Hoop Jr. cool out, he was heard to say, "I never thought I'd make it this quick."

Hooper was from Jacksonville, Florida, and he had spent most of his life in contracting and cattle breeding. He came to the sales at Keeneland in 1943 to get into racing and Hoop Jr. was the first yearling he bought paying $10,200 from the consignment of Robert A. Fairbairn from Winchester, Kentucky. Fairbairn's farm manager was Carter Thornton, who had earlier sold Gallahadion also bred by Fairbairn, as a yearling and, at a sale a few years later, handled the sale of yet another Kentucky Derby winner, Canonero II. The 1943 sale was the first sale scheduled at Keeneland. Because of the war, the sales at Saratoga were canceled, and Fasig Tipton made the decision to have a sale of yearlings from Kentucky and Tennessee at Keeneland. A tent was erected in the paddock and this was the beginning of the Breeders' Sales Company, which evolved into the sales governed by the Keeneland Association.

Getting back to the Derby, Hoop Jr., breaking from post position 12, broke in front and opened a clear lead, was six in front at the eighth pole and won by six over Pot O' Luck, with Darby Dieppe third. Arcaro was aboard Hoop Jr. for his third Derby win. He had won with Whirlaway in 1941 and with Lawrin in 1938, both trained by Ben Jones. Hoop Jr. paid $9.40. I couldn't afford to bet on my half-dollar weekly allowance, and Dad wouldn't have trusted my handicapping anyway. But, as a lad, picking a Kentucky Derby winner was good for my ego.

Hoop Jr. was by Sir Gallahad III out of the high-class stakes winner One Hour, by Snob II. She won the Beldame, Adirondack and Hiawatha Handicap and produced twelve winners from fourteen foals—four stakes winners, including a full brother to Hoop Jr. named the Sir Jeffrey. She also was the ancestress of many stakes winners, among them some that may ring the bell of old-timers, including Victory Morn, Battle Morn, Amber Morn and the high-class handicap mare Politely.

The Kentucky Derby was Hoop Jr.'s last hurrah. His next start was in the Preakness and he bowed a tendon and finished second to Polynesian after making a strong bid, only to drop back suddenly to be beaten by two and a half lengths. Plans were made to retire him to stud at Dr. Charles E. Hagyard's Greenridge Farm near Lexington, but that fell through. He left no record at stud.

REIGH COUNT, COUNT FLEET, COUNT TURF

The 1928 winner of the Kentucky Derby was Reigh Count, a chestnut colt by imported Sun Reigh out of imported Contessina, by Count Schomberg, bred by Willis Sharpe Kilmer. The crop of 1925 was considered to be one of the best of all time until the crop of 1954 arrived. The latter crop included Bold Ruler, Round Table, Gallant Man and Iron Liege.

Reigh Count was not the leading two-year-old of his year. The leader was the ill-fated Dice. Dice, a son of Dominant bred by H.P. Whitney and sold to the Wheatley Stable, was undefeated in his first four starts—carrying 127 pounds on one occasion—but he died suddenly due to an internal hemorrhage. Reigh Count developed slowly, and it took him seven tries before he broke his maiden. John Hertz happened to be at the races one day at Saratoga and watched Reigh Count savage his rival when he lapped him in the final yards of a race. That impressed Hertz so much that he bought Reigh Count for $15,000 from Kilmer. Reigh Count won the one-mile Kentucky Jockey Club Stakes and the Walden Stakes and ended up rated second only to Dice at two. Others in his crop were Ariel (later a noted source of speed), Toro, Misstep, Victorian, Genie and Petee-Wrack, plus the high-class fillies Glade, Anita Peabody and Bateau, a daughter of Man o' War bred by Walter Jeffords.

Reigh Count was generally considered to be the best three-year-old in 1928. He was almost invincible. After winning an allowance race in his first start, he won the Kentucky Derby by a length over Misstep and Toro, going from the four slot in a field of twenty-two, the largest in Derby history. He then won the Miller Stakes, caught the mud and ran out of the money in the Travers, his only bad race of the year, then closed out the season with wins in the Huron Stakes, Saratoga Cup in record time, the Realization and the Jockey Club Gold Cup.

Unraced at four, Reigh Count entered stud at Hertz's Stoner Creek Farm, and in 1939 Hertz sent the mare Quickly to be bred to him. The result of that mating was one of the all-time greats, Count Fleet, winner of the Triple Crown in 1943. Quickly never won or placed in stakes but she won thirty-two races so she was better than an empty stall. She also was the dam of Depth Charge, who had so much speed he was much in demand by breeders of quarter horses.

Count Fleet was ranked fifth behind Man o' War, Secretariat, Citation and Kelso in *Thoroughbred Champions: Top 100 Racehorses of the 20ᵗʰ Century*, published by the *Blood-Horse*. Love that book! Years ago, I was invited to participate with the late John H. "Trader" Clark in a radio tribute to the best horse we had ever seen compete. Clark named Count Fleet. I said Secretariat, although I had a nagging doubt there. I had watched Swaps run on the West Coast and he made moves that gave you chill bumps. Swaps was ranked twentieth on the list, so I guess John was right.

I always had a couple of questions about Count Fleet. Occupation had beaten him twice as a two-year-old, and he never ran again after the Belmont Stakes. There was no question about his ability as a sire. He ranked number one on both the sire list and the broodmare sire list; in fact, one of his daughters produced Kelso, who ranked fourth among the all-time great runners of the twentieth century, just above his grandsire, Count Fleet.

I had a chance to see Count Fleet—I think it was in either 1949 or 1950. He did not make a big impression at the time. I was working part-time at Dixiana and had the task of taking a mare to be bred to him, Early Blossom, I believe. She was a daughter of Bimelech. She never produced anything of note.

In 1947, Dr. Frank P. Miller of Riverside, California, sent a mare named Delmarie to be bred to Count Fleet. She was by Pompey out of a daughter of Polymelian, which sounds good, but the female family was rather weak. By the time Delmarie was through producing, it was a heck of a lot stronger. Anyway, she got in foal and was either left in Kentucky or returned in time for Count Turf's birth because he was still in Kentucky until he was weaned and then returned to California. His next trip was to Saratoga, where New Yorker Jack Amiel bought him for $3,700.

Amiel ran a restaurant called the Turf Restaurant in New York and later was the managing partner in Jack Dempsey's popular watering hole. When the time came he turned the horse over to trainer Sol Rutchick, who had a public stable based at the old Jamaica Race Track. Rutchick won the Dover Stakes with him as a two-year-old and kept him mostly in sprints. Count Turf had developed a habit of bearing out and Rutchick put blinkers on him, coupled with a severe bit, to correct the habit. This did not pay off. He had won but one six-furlong sprint going into the Derby.

Entered for the Wood Memorial, Count Turf got off poorly, and while he didn't finish in the money, he made a nice closing run. This convinced Amiel that the colt wanted to come from behind and he asked Rutchick to send him to Kentucky. Rutchick refused.

Count Turf had been galloped in the mornings by Conn McCreary, a noted come-from-behind rider who had fallen on hard times. McCreary had won the 1944 Kentucky Derby on Calumet's Pensive but by the time he took Count Turf to the track he had won but four races all year. Amiel had watched McCreary on Count Turf in the morning and noted that the horse got along with him very well, so he went to see him. He asked McCreary if he would ride Count Turf in the Kentucky Derby. McCreary asked if he was serious about going to Kentucky. Amiel replied, "Only if you ride him."

When Amiel told Rutchick his plan, Rutchick said he didn't want any part of it. Count Turf arrived in Kentucky by plane two weeks before the Derby. Rutchick stayed in New York and sent his assistant, Gene Sully. The first thing McCreary did when Count Turf went out on the Churchill track to gallop was to say, "Take the blinkers and that bit off. All I want is the simple D bit." The horse galloped like a charm.

One morning, Count Turf worked a mile in 1:38 and 4/5, a very good move. When Rutchick heard about it, he called Amiel wanting to send a "good rider." Amiel said no. On the day before the Derby, the colt worked a half in :45 and 4.

Count Turf had drawn post position nine in a field of twenty. He was a member of the mutual field with Phil D, Pur Sang, King Clover and Fighting Back. In those days of "mutual fields," if any of the five won you could cash your ticket, and the odds were 14–1. Count Turf broke well, was rated in about the middle of the pack, moved to sixth after three quarters in 1:12 and 2/5, was up to fourth after a mile in 1:37, took the lead at the head of the stretch and won going away by four lengths.

That was Count Turf's only win as a three-year-old. The following year, he won one race; at five, he won the Questionnaire Handicap and finished third in the Massachusetts, Queens County and Valley Forge Handicaps with a record of eight wins, four seconds, six thirds and earnings of $166,375. He accomplished nothing at stud.

Delmarie's pedigree looked pretty good on paper after Count Turf's Derby score. She also was the dam of Golden Briar, a colt by Centime that won twenty races, including stakes; Good Gesture, a full brother to Count Turf that also won twenty races and placed in the Myrtlewood Handicap; and two daughters that became stakes producers.

TOMY LEE

One of the most exciting Kentucky Derbys I have seen was the 1959 edition won by Tomy Lee. I left Dixiana the previous year to go to work at the

Blood-Horse and bummed a ride to Louisville with Skeets Meadows, a local photographer and good guy. Skeets had a new car, and as I recall, it was a Ford. He didn't have much respect for speed limits. The trip to Louisville was fine, but the return trip was something else again! Skeets had a couple of hummers in him, and I think it was about that time that I started to lose my hair. I was sure glad to get back safely to his studio on Third Street in Lexington. Skeets passed away many moons ago, and his collection of photographs is now at the Keeneland Library.

Getting back to Tomy Lee, I first saw him at Keeneland prior to the Derby. It was Blue Grass Stakes day, and I walked into the paddock where he was being saddled. There was a big crowd around him, and all I could see was his head, with ears pricked, looking out over the crowd as if they were not there. You know the look. The look of eagles. I turned around and walked back to the grandstand and bet five dollars to win on him, saving enough to buy a cup of burgoo. He won, of course, beating Dunce, a son of Tom Fool, with Scotland, a colt by Princequillo, third.

At Churchill Downs with Skeets I had a chance to really inspect Tomy Lee. He was bay, about 16 hands, small star, white on all four and very light bone. He was owned by Frank Turner Jr. of Midland, Texas, and trained by Frank Childs. Childs said he had never seen a horse with more speed, "If he was never asked to race beyond a mile he would be unbeatable." And he darn near was unbeatable as a two-year-old, winning his first six starts, including the Del Mar Futurity, Starlet, Charles S. Howard and Haggin Stakes. He came East and was a supplementary nominee to the Champagne Stakes. Shoemaker had been his regular rider in California but Hartack had the mount for the Champagne. Childs told him, "This horse can go to the front or rate just off the pace," but Hartack took him back and he was beaten by a neck by First Landing. Two weeks later, in the rich Garden State Stakes, Tomy Lee drew the eleventh post position, lost a lot of ground on the first turn and got to the lead down the backside but he couldn't hold off First Landing and was beaten by a neck again. That decided champion two-year-old colt honors, with the laurels going to First Landing, who raced for Meadows Stable. Childs was not too happy about that. "We'll be gunning for him next year."

Turner had purchased Tomy Lee as a weanling in England. He had acquired an agent to buy a weanling colt by Tulyar out of a mare that had won the Irish Two Thousand Guineas, then instructed him to buy a colt by Tutor Minstrel as a traveling companion. The Tulyar colt, later named Tuleg, cost him about $25,000, the Tutor Minstrel colt that turned out to be

Tomy Lee, $6,762. Tuleg injured his shoulder shortly after arriving in this country and never raced, but Turner hit the jackpot with Tomy Lee. "That name just popped into my head," Turner related. "I had been turned down on so many requests for names that I thought I would have a better chance of having the name approved if I spelled it with one 'm'."

It's interesting that the one-two-three finishers in the Garden State were the first three finishers in the Kentucky Derby months later. First Landing was the slight favorite, going off at $3.60 to 1, Tomy Lee at $3.70 to 1. Sword Dancer went off at $8.80 to 1. The race turned into a dog fight between Tomy Lee and Brookmeade Stables' Sword Dancer. Tomy Lee forced the early pace set by Troilus, who gave it up after six furlongs. Tomy Lee put his head in front at that point and, a few strides later, was joined by Sword Dancer. Sword Dancer had a slight lead after a mile, and from that point on, the two were locked together. Tomy Lee was on the inside and was drifting out slightly under Bill Shoemaker with Sword Dancer lugging in so there was contact throughout the length of the stretch. Someone wrote that Tomy Lee was tiring and that Sword Dancer, by brushing him, had made him change leads and that cost Sword Dancer the race. All I know is that when they hit the wire, Tomy Lee's nose was in front. Fantastic race. Took your breath away. Bill Boland, who was aboard Sword Dancer, claimed foul after the race, but it was disallowed. On the cover of the *Blood-Horse* was a picture of Tomy Lee draped in the garland of roses, and the caption read, "Roses are for Courage."

Tomy Lee went on to win a couple of more races but never won another stakes. Childs was quoted as saying that because of his light frame he was not the type that could stand a lot of usage. All I know is that on the first Saturday of May 1959 I was privileged to have witnessed a display of courage only to be found in the Thoroughbred. Years later, I stumbled across this poem written by J.A. Joe Estes and published in the May 16, 1931 issue of the *Blood-Horse*, and Tomy Lee immediately came to mind:

REUNION

Trooping again to the Downs today, to the city at the
Falls,
And the North comes, and the East comes, and the West
when the Derby calls,
With the old South and the new South and the fair
South meeting,

The glad hand, and the true smile, and the wide armed
greeting,
A gay throng, and a glad throng, from many lands
they hail,
But the Downs has made them one today at the end of
the Derby trail,
And the rich are there, and the much too poor, all the
wide earth's breeding,
And the Derby field parading by, with a proud horse
leading.
And the many colored jackets fill in the warm South's
breeze,
The green and the wine dark purple, and the lavender
sash and cerise;
But the track is wide, and side by side with that proud
crew striding
Is a ghostly throng that floats along, with a little red
horse guiding.
Trooping again to the Downs today, out of old history's
stalls,
Trooping out of the living past, they hear when the
Derby calls.
What is it you say? You don't see them?—Is it just
my dreaming—
Those restive steeds with the bright flanks and the
great eyes gleaming!
Trooping back to the Downs today, the phantom field
is there,
Back to the Downs their ghosts have come, to greet
the one to wear
The derby wreath when the day is done, and give him
fellow greeting—
For none wear that but the strong of limb, them with
the stout heart beating.

Tomy Lee was retired to stud at Lou Doherty and Harold Snowden's Stallion Station on Russell Cave Pike, property now owned by Kenny McPeek, but he proved to be virtually sterile siring but three or four foals. He's buried there.

Sword Dancer and First Landing went on to greater glory. Sword Dancer ran second in the Preakness to Royal Orbit, a colt by Royal Charger that had run fourth in the Kentucky Derby. Sword Dancer then won the Metropolitan, the Belmont Stakes over Bagdad and Royal Orbit and the Monmouth Handicap from Americo. Sword Dancer was beaten by three parts of a length by Babu in the Brooklyn Handicap, giving him ten pounds, then closed out the year with wins in the Travers, over Middle Brother, the Woodward by a head from Hillsdale with Round Table third, and a seven-length score over Round Table in the two-mile Jockey Club Gold Cup to lock up not only the three-year-old championship but Horse of the Year as well.

Sword Dancer came back at four to win several more stakes. His first win of the season came in the Grey Lag at Aqueduct when he gave his old rival First Landing two pounds and beat him by a neck. They met again in the Suburban, and this time Sword Dancer's margin of victory was a half length while giving him four pounds. His final stakes win came in the Woodward, and he closed his career with a third in the Man o' War on the grass. He had tried the grass twice before, with his best a second in the United Nations Handicap to T.V. Lark. Sword Dancer retired with a record of fifteen wins, seven seconds and four thirds and earnings of $826,610 before being sent to Claiborne Farm.

Sword Dancer was by Sunglow, a son of Sun Again standing at Mereworth Farm. Sunglow won the Discovery, Saranac and Widener Handicaps and the Chesapeake Stakes but sired just six stakes winners. Sword Dancer's dam was Highland Fling, by By Jimminy, and he was her only stakes winner. Sword Dancer sired eleven stakes winners and may have outbred himself by siring Horse of the Year Damascus. He also was the sire of the champion filly Lady Pitt. Sword Dancer passed away in 1984.

First Landing made a game try in the Derby, finishing third, beaten by a bit over two lengths for all the money, but two weeks later he threw in a clunker in the Preakness, finishing ninth, beaten by sixteen lengths by Royal Orbit. First Landing was rested for some five months, returning to win back-to-back allowance races at Aqueduct. His first try in a stakes following the Preakness was in the Roamer on November 3 and he was beaten by a nose by Polylad while giving him eleven pounds. Four days later First Landing ran out of the money in the Trenton Handicap over a muddy surface to end his three-year-old season.

First Landing next appeared on January 8, 1960, at Santa Anita winning an overnight handicap going a mile and a sixteenth and winning by a half length. Four days later he was a pacesetting second, beaten by a half length in the San Fernando Stakes. He then posted his first stakes win of the year in the Santa Anita Maturity, a race restricted to four-year-olds. He made two more starts on the West Coast before returning East, a second to Bagdad in the San Antonio and a no factor performance in the Santa Anita Handicap won by Linmold.

First Landing was to make nine more starts before retiring with a record of nineteen wins, nine seconds and two thirds for earnings of $779,577. He won the Laurel Maturity beating Calumet's On and On and the Monmouth Handicap; he was beaten by Sword Dancer in both the Grey Lag and the Suburban and by Bald Eagle in the Metropolitan. In his final start and first try on the turf, he finished ninth in the United Nations Handicap won by T.V. Lark.

First Landing, like Sword Dancer, was retired to stud at Claiborne Farm and finally got the best of his old rival by siring twenty-seven stakes winners. His best was Riva Ridge, winner of the 1972 Kentucky Derby, carrying the silks of C.T. Chenery of the Meadow Stud. Riva Ridge wired the field that day, leading at every call to win with relative ease over No Le Hace and Hold Your Peace. Years later, in an interview with Penny Chenery while she was living in Lexington, I asked if her father was aware that he had won the Derby with Riva Ridge, knowing that he was incapacitated at the time and approaching his final days. "Oh yes," she replied, "the lady who was caring for him at the time watched the race on the TV with my father and when Riva Ridge won she turned and said, 'Mr. Chenery you just won the Kentucky Derby,' and there were tears in his eyes." It took me a moment to recover from that one.

I had been at Churchill Downs to watch the Derby, and the word was out that they had a colt in the stable that would make you forget about Riva Ridge. That, of course, was Secretariat, yet to make his first start as a two-year-old.

8

At the Sales

REVOKED

One of the top two-year-olds of 1945 was Revoked. Revoked was bred by Dr. Eslie Asbury and raised at his Forest Retreat Farm near Carlisle, Kentucky. He was a dark bay with no white markings and was offered at the 1944 Keeneland Summer Sales. He was by the popular and successful Blue Larkspur out of the Sir Galahad III mare Gala Belle. Gala Belle had placed in stakes and had already produced a stakes winner in Alabama, a colt by Mahmoud that had won the Ral Parr Stakes and finished second in the Mayflower and the Bay Shore. Revoked was a good-looking colt, expected to sell well, and he did, going to the successful owner/trainer Max Hirsch for $41,000. Hirsch trained for a number of owners but indicated that this one was for himself.

The colt was vanned over to Hartland Stud in Woodford County and turned out. When he ran in the paddock, he made some sort of noise that made Hirsch think he might have a wind problem, and a couple of days after the sale he notified the sales company that he was going to have it checked out by a veterinarian. The first to check Revoked out reported that the "nasal" sounds were only noticed upon exhalation, but not inhalations. Another vet was called, same diagnosis. "I don't want to know anything about inhalation and outhalation, I just want to know, is he sound in the wind?" Hirsch demanded.

The opinions of three more veterinarians came with various results; one said, "This colt's breathing may improve with work but I'm inclined to believe that in time he will be a pronounced roarer." Hirsch notified the sales company that he refused to take the colt for $41,000.

Max Hirsch could hardly be blamed for refusing to take a colt for that amount of money—remember this was 1946, without thorough assurance that the colt was sound in wind, and the examinations were done in the era before endoscopes were available and had left the question open. Dr. Asbury offered to make the sale conditional on the ultimate soundness of wind of the colt. This seemed fair, and had the colt sold for $5,000 or so it would probably have been accepted. But what if some injury had happened to further confuse the mix-up? Dr. Asbury settled the matter by notifying the Breeders' Sales Company that he would take the colt back. On August 21, some five weeks after the sale, Revoked was returned to Forest Retreat.

Aptly named Revoked was sent to the Lexington trotting track, the "Red Mile," to be cared for by Hunter Moody, who broke him to a sulky. I guess Dr. Asbury decided that having gone this far with the colt he was going to hang in there. Then Revoked was turned over for more serious training to Howard "Babe" Wells of Lexington, and he was taken to Keeneland around March then sent to Arlington Park.

Revoked made his first start on July 26 with jockey Al Bodiou aboard. He broke in a tangle, straightened out, then ran by the field to win by three. On August 4, he won his second start in a race for non-winners of two by four with speed in reserve. Nine days later he opened the lead but was caught at the wire to be beaten by a neck by Inroc, a very fast colt that later developed into an outstanding sprinter. Revoked had gone the first quarter in :22 and 1/5, which may have been the reason for his late defeat.

Five days later he went to the post for the Washington Park Futurity. Dixiana's undefeated colt, Spy Song, was the favorite, but he was eliminated early in the race after being kicked in the knee behind the starting gate. This ended his season. Revoked drew away at the eighth pole to win by four, with Safe Reward making a late run to best Fighting Frank for second. The race was worth $56,700 to the winner, and Dr. Asbury was in front. Later in the season, Revoked ran second in the Cowden and third in the Hopeful to end the year with three wins, two seconds and a third from six starts.

Revoked did not race well at three, winning but one race and finishing second in the Hawthorne Sprint. Retired to stud at Forest Retreat, he sired twenty-six stakes winners, including the champion filly Furl Sail. She was bred by E.K. Thomas, owner of Timberlawn Farm in Bourbon County, and she was out of Windsail, a stakes-placed daughter of Count Fleet. Windsail also produced the good handicap horse Super Sail, by To Market.

Revoked sired another stakes winner that I liked named Reneged. Reneged was a hard-hitting runner that went to stud at the Nuckols brothers' Hurstland Farm on the outskirts of Midway, Kentucky. He was a foal of 1953 and, I believe, stood for $1,000. Couldn't have been much more than that because that was about all I could afford. I had purchased a mare named Vina off the track, bred her to Reneged and sold her in foal. The resulting foal was named Renewed Vigor, and he won the Equipoise Mile at Arlington. Another high-class runner by Revoked was Rejected. He won the Santa Anita Handicap, Hollywood Gold Cup and a number of other stakes and earned over $500,000 for King Ranch. He could run all day.

DETERMINE

In 1952, history came close to repeating for Dr. Asbury. He offered a dark gray colt by Alibhai out of Koubis, by Mahmoud, at the Keeneland Summer Sales, and Californian Andrew Crevolin bought him for $12,000. After signing the ticket, he turned to the doctor and said, "Why did you let me buy that colt? I must've been standing in a hole when I looked at him." Dr. Asbury told him, "If you don't like him, I'll give you $15,000 for him right now." Crevolin decided to keep him. Maybe he had heard the tale of Revoked. Two years later the colt, named Determine, won the Kentucky Derby. Determine's dam, Koubis, was born with a cleft palate that Dr. Asbury surgically repaired using existing medical instruments that he had personally modified and elongated in his workshop to be able to reach and surgically repair the cleft.

Crevolin was right about the size of the colt. At Derby time, Determine stood 15 hands and weighed 975 pounds. He was big enough though. Breaking from post position seven in the seventeen-horse field, he stalked the early pace of the high-class colt Hasty Road, who went on to win the Preakness, and ran him down in the stretch to win by a length and a half. Walmac Farm's Hassayampa finished third with some pretty good colts behind them, Correlation, Fisherman, Goyamo and Admiral Porter among them.

Determine returned to California and competed through his four-year-old season. At career's end he had won sixteen stakes and earned $573,360.

Retired to stud, he did quite well, siring twenty stakes winners, including champion two-year-old Warfare and the 1962 Kentucky Derby winner Decidedly.

Decidedly was bred by G.A. Pope Jr. and foaled at his El Peco Ranch near Madera, California. He was raced by Pope and trained by Horatio Luro and had finished second to Ridan in the Blue Grass Stakes. The pre-race favorite for the Derby was C.T. Chenery's Sir Gaylord, by Turn-To, trained by Casey Hayes. The morning before the Derby, Sir Gaylord pulled up lame. A few years back, in an interview, Penny Chenery talked about Sir Gaylord: "Dad decided that we would retire Sir Gaylord to stud. We had entered both Sir Gaylord and Cicada in the Derby with Cicada also entered in the Oaks. Some discussion was made about running her in the Derby but instead Casey, an old-time trainer, said he had already pulled her hay and she knew she was to run that day so the decision was made for her to go in the Oaks." Cicada, a daughter of Brian G and Satsuma, by Bossuet, won by three over Flaming Page and Fortunate Isle and went on to be named champion three-year-old filly. Sir Gaylord went to stud at Claiborne Farm.

Don't know how Sir Gaylord would've run in the Derby, but it would've taken a heckuva horse to beat Decidedly that day. He won by two and a quarter lengths and set a new track record of 2:00 and 2/5, a full second faster than Whirlaway's 2:01 and 2/5 set in 1941. Running second was T.A. Grissom's Roman Line, with Ridan third, having washed out badly hearing the band play "Dixie" on the walk over. Sunrise County, Crimson Satan, Admirals Voyage and others trailed them home.

Roman Line ran a game race in the Derby. His time would have won a lot of them. He was a good four lengths out of it turning for home, stuck his head in front at the eighth pole and finished a neck in front of Ridan to be second. He went off at 23–1, largely because, I suspect, he was by Roman and many thought he would never get a mile and a quarter. They should've checked out his dam, Lurline B. She won the nine-furlong Santa Margarita and set a new track record for a mile and three quarters at Del Mar.

Lurline B. was a foal of 1945 by Alibhi out of Belle Cane, by Beau Pere, and she produced four stakes winners for Grissom. The first was Guide Line, a filly by Nasrullah. She won the Selima Stakes as a two-year-old. Lurullah, also by Nasrullah, won the Sheridan Handicap and Michigan Derby. Roman Line won the Breeders' Futurity and set a new track record for five furlongs at Churchill at two. At three, he was third in the Bluegrass, ran second in the Louisiana Derby, won the Derby Trial and, of course, was second in the Kentucky Derby and third in the Preakness and Blue

Grass Stakes. Lurline B.'s fourth stakes winner was City Line, and I have a little tale to tell about him.

I was visiting Grissom at his Duntreath Farm, which was located on the Paris Pike just north of Muir Station Road. This was just a couple of weeks before the July Summer Sale at Keeneland. We walked out to a paddock, and there was a chestnut colt stretched out in the middle of the paddock sound asleep. So we opened the gate and walked out to get a good look at him. Well, we got within about ten yards of him and must've startled him because he was up and gone faster than a scalded cat! Unbelievably quick. Grissom said, "If he can get out of the starting gate that fast, he's going to win some races."

A friend of mine, Alan F. Brewer Jr., had been asked by a lady from Canada to buy her a yearling out of the sale. I told him to take a look at the Windy City II colt that Grissom had in the sale. He went for something else, and Grissom bought the colt back for, as I recall, $18,000. Grissom named him City Line, and he won the Louisiana Derby, Le Compte Handicap and Detroit Sweepstakes with him.

Speaking of Alan Brewer, he was a well-known artist back then. The best thing he ever did was a conformation painting of Man o' War that used to hang in the lobby of the *Blood-Horse* magazine when it was located in Gardenside in Lexington. He called my Dad once about something or other, and when Dad picked up the phone, he said, "This is Alan Brewer, the painter." Dad replied, "Glad you called, because I need some fences done." Alan was laughing when he told me about that, so he could take a joke. I guess Dad was joking. Alan tragically died in the crash of a private plane on his way to see the Washington, D.C. International at Laurel in 1967.

9

Growing Up on the Russell Cave Pike

DIXIANA

I was blessed to grow up on Dixiana Farm. Dixiana is located about seven miles north of Lexington on Russell Cave Pike. The entrance is right across the road from the cave itself. The cave served as a gathering place for political debates in the old days, and it was there that prior to the Civil War famed abolitionist Cassius Clay was involved in an incident that resulted in the death of a paid assassin. The assassin had been sent by proslavery proponents, and he fired a pistol at Clay. The bullet struck a bowie knife that Clay always carried and was deflected. Clay drew the knife, cut the assassin's throat and threw his body into the stream that flows from the cave. Many years later, when I was in the fourth grade at Russell Cave Elementary, a friend of mine was killed in the cave when a large section of the ceiling fell on him, breaking his neck. I haven't been back since.

The entrance to the cave is barely visible from the road, even though it is large enough to pull a semi truck in if you could get to it. As you face the cave, there is a stream flowing from the left side that in normal conditions is but four or five feet wide, but with heavy rains, it floods. I would estimate that the entrance is about ten to fifteen yards wide and extends approximately twenty yards deep, then narrows, so one must stoop to proceed. That was about as far as I had the guts to go, and I know of no one who has gone farther.

Partially blocking the view from the road is the stone building that used to house the system that furnished water to the house and the swimming pool on Mt. Brilliant Farm. I don't know if it supplied water to the rest of the farm, but I know darn well about the pool. Early in the summer it was ice cold. Dive in and you came up whooping! Mrs. Haggin would occasionally come and watch us swim. Lovely lady. She thought that Jimmy Hutchins, who also lived on Dixiana, was my brother, and if we failed to show up to swim after several days, she would call my mother and ask "if the boys were all right."

Grover Hughes, my schoolmate who was killed in the cave, had several brothers who later became trainers: Donald, Lawrence and Leonard. The family had a farm on Russell Cave Pike closer to Lexington.

We moved from the Iron Works Pike property to Dixiana in 1937. There were some 1,200 acres, plenty of room to roam and to ride. My two favorite mounts were Sweetheart, a Tennessee Walker, and Yellow Kid. Yellow Kid was off the racetrack, where he had been used as a lead pony, but I suspect that he had spent some time on a ranch. We had a nice-sized herd of Hereford cattle on the farm. From time to time, they had to be moved from one field to another. I would ride the Yellow Kid and he made me look good. All I had to do was hang on, and he knew exactly what to do. What fun! During the war, that would be World War II, we also raised tobacco and hemp.

The farm was divided into sections, one for Thoroughbreds and the other for Saddlebred show horses. Mary Fisher, everyone called her Miss Mary, was deeply involved with the show horses. She rode sidesaddle, and the office was loaded with trophies and ribbons she had won. I have my suspicions about the show horses, though. One of the Dixiana three gated champions, Royal Irish, was scheduled to compete in the American Saddlebred World Championship at the Kentucky State Fair in Louisville. A few days before the show, a truckload of sheep arrived at the farm. Now the Fishers never raised sheep, but it turned out the judge at the state fair did. Dad said to Mom, "Let's drive down and watch Royal Irish win." They did, and he did, and the sheep soon departed. Maybe things have changed, but since the sheep incident, I have thought that racing was more on the up and up.

In 1947, Dixiana held a dispersal sale of the show horses. Miss Mary had been won over by the Thoroughbreds and remained so the rest of her life, taking over the farm after her father passed away in 1963. She could really ride, looked great on a horse competing sidesaddle. The family would go to the Junior League Horse Show every summer at the Red Mile trotting track in Lexington to cheer her on. I was in awe of her as a kid, but as I grew up to where she could tolerate me, we became good friends. I still miss her.

I could not write anything about growing up without telling you about the Jot 'Em Down Store. The Jot 'Em Down was founded in the early 1930s by Lucian and Edward Terrell, and it was named after a radio show popular at the time. I remember it as a general store where you could buy your overalls, work shirts, galoshes and other stuff like that. I had my first taste of ice cream at the Jot 'Em Down. The story goes that I was about three or four, and Dad bought me an ice cream cone. Guess I didn't know what to do with it. Dad was talking, looked down at me, and there I was with melting ice cream dripping off my elbow. "Hell, boy, eat that damn thing." The Terrells loved to tell that story.

Mrs. Terrell, Dolly, was like a second mother to me. They had three kids: Bob, Lucian and Frances. Bob later played baseball for the University of Kentucky and went into the U.S. Air Force. He had about one hundred solo hours while stationed in Texas, but when they found out he was a darn good third baseman, he spent the rest of his enlistment on the camp baseball team. Lucian became my best friend; in fact, he was best man at my wedding, and I was best man at his.

The kids called Uncle Edward "Goo Goo," and Goo Goo was quite a character. They sold gas at the time, Texaco, and of course, it was quite cheap. Goo Goo had a chair behind the Warm Morning stove, and if somebody pulled up wanting gas, he would holler, "How much do you want?" If it was under a dollar, he'd holler, "Go on into town and get it." His best one came when they were doing inventory one day. They ran across an item that obviously had been selling real well. "Hell," said Goo Goo, "don't order any more of that stuff, we can't keep it in stock."

The Jot 'Em Down is still in business and it's owned by Robbie Terrell, the founder's grandson. They no longer sell dry goods or gas, but you can get a heckuva cheeseburger there and the TV is always on the racing channel.

I also had a good buddy, Jimmy Hutchins, whose father was the maintenance manager at Dixiana, and he lived just a field away on the farm. We ran around together a lot, would go swimming in Mrs. Haggin's pool on Mount Brilliant Farm across the road or go to Joyland, an amusement park near Lexington. I recall fixing the Easter Egg hunt at the Mount Horeb Presbyterian Church when Jimmy and I were about nine or ten. The prize was for the winner with the most eggs and one for the person with the fewest eggs. We figured that out real quick. I gave all my eggs to Jimmy, and he won a big basket full of goodies. I got a yo-yo.

Now, you knew they knew what was going on but, being good Christians, said nothing.

Jimmy was quite an athlete. He was all-state in basketball and baseball, was given a basketball scholarship to Western Kentucky, hated it, transferred to Transylvania and was all-conference three straight years. He also played the guitar and the harmonica, and the girls followed him around. It was tough growing up with Jimmy.

ALLEGRO AND JOHNSTOWN

I have a beautiful color photograph of Allegro taken in the post parade at Keeneland in 1938. He carries the Dixiana silks, solferino, buff sash and scarlet cap. Don't ask about solferino, looks maroon to me. A few decades later, when my wife, Jackie, applied for racing silks, she chose scarlet and buff stripes with the scarlet cap. No solferino.

Allegro was a gelded son of High Time out of Brenda, by Johren, and he met Belair Stud's Johnstown in the 1937 Breeder's Futurity. Johnstown went in the race off a seven-length Remsen win at Jamaica, and he was the heavy favorite. The two were head to head at the eighth pole, they hit the wire the same way. There was no photo-finish camera at that time and the judges gave the nod to Johnstown. The official chart of the race gives the margin of victory as a nose.

Well, a few days later a guy stopped by the office at Dixiana to see Dad. He had taken a picture of the finish and in the picture the nose belonged to Allegro. Now I know about camera angles—how in the world could a guy with an old-fashioned camera catch them at the exact moment they hit the wire? But Dad went to his grave believing that Allegro had won.

Allegro won four stakes for Dixiana and it was surely no disgrace to be beaten by Johnstown. Johnstown was bred by A.B. Hancock Sr., owner of Ellerslie Stud in Virginia and Claiborne Farm in Kentucky, where he was to stand at stud. He raced in the silks of William Woodward's Belair Stud. The Woodwards bred and raised many great horses, including Gallant Fox and Omaha, the only father-son winners of the Triple Crown.

Johnstown won seven of his twelve starts as a two-year-old and four stakes, and he concluded the year with three straight stakes wins. He extended his win streak to seven as a three-year-old, winning, in order, the Paumonok Handicap, an allowance race, the Wood Memorial, all three at Jamaica,

Allegro at Keeneland. *Blythe photo, 1939.*

then shipped to Churchill Downs to win the Kentucky Derby by an eye-popping eight lengths over Challedon, a colt later considered by many to be the best ever foaled in Maryland. Seven days later he threw in a clunker, tiring badly to finish fifth of six in the Preakness, beaten by eleven lengths.

The Derby was run on May 6, the Preakness on May 13, and he stopped badly to be out of the money. Trainer Sonny Jim Fitzsimmons sent him to the post for the May 27 running of the one-mile Withers Stakes. He won by five. Seven days later, he won the mile-and-a-half Belmont Stakes by five and two weeks after that the nine-furlong Dwyer by a length. That was his last win. Somewhere down the line he developed a breathing problem. Sent to Chicago, he tired badly to be beaten by some six lengths by Challedon in the Classic and was retired. Challedon went on to be named champion three-year-old.

Johnstown was sent back to Claiborne Farm for stud duties where he was a bit of a disappointment. His main claim to fame was that he was the broodmare sire of champion Nashua, a son of Nasrullah that also raced for the Woodward family. He also was the broodmare sire of To Market, who did very well at stud while standing at Claiborne Farm.

To digress, which I am wont to do, Challedon also retired to stud in Kentucky, going to Ira Drymon's Gallagher Farm on Russell Cave Pike. After his win over Johnstown in the Classic in Chicago, he ran second in a stakes at Narragansett then won his last six starts to wind up his three-year-old season. All six were stakes: the Narragansett Special, Hawthorne Gold Cup, Havre de Grace Handicap, Tranter Stakes at Keeneland, Maryland Handicap and the Pimlico Special, besting the four-year-old Kayak II, winner earlier that year of the Santa Anita Handicap.

As a four-year-old in 1940, Challedon won five of his seven starts, including the Whitney, Hollywood Gold Cup, Havre de Grace Handicap and Pimlico Special; ran second to Hash in the Narragansett Special, giving him eight pounds; and finished third to Eight Thirty and Hash in the Massachusetts Handicap, giving them four and fifteen pounds, respectively.

Challedon was to run sixteen more times at five and six posting but two wins and one stakes win, that in the Philadelphia Handicap at Havre de Grace, and that was a shame. Obviously past his prime, it tarnished his reputation and harmed his popularity when he was retired. He was moderately successful, siring Kentucky Oaks winner Challe Ann, the full brothers Tenacious and Gigantic that dominated at the Fair Grounds for Joe W. Brown of Lexington, Hollywood Oaks winner Mrs. Fuddy, champion steeplechaser Ancestor and one of my all-time favorites, Shy Guy.

Shy Guy was bred by Mary V. Fisher, Miss Mary to all, and he was no shy guy. Don't know why Miss Mary chose that name for him, because Shy Guy was as tough as nails. He won fifteen races for Dixiana, seven stakes, and placed in fifteen other stakes. He won the 1947 renewal of Keeneland's Breeders Futurity, the Louisville Handicap and the Keeneland Special. But the race that sticks out in my mind is the seventy-fifth running of the Clark Handicap at Churchill Downs.

The Clark was run over a mile and a sixteenth and Shy Guy faced the formidable entry of Calumet Farm's Free America and Armed. Calumet, for you youngsters, dominated racing back in the 1940s. Shy Guy was assigned top weight of 123 pounds, with Conn McCreary aboard. Armed, under Gordon Glisson, carried 120, and Free America was ridden by America's premier rider, Eddie Arcaro, 118.

Armed took the lead and was in front after a half, with Shy Guy pushing the pace a half length in front of Free America. Shy Guy took the lead after three quarters, with Free America a half length back in second. By the eighth pole the lead was still a half length, with Arcaro going to the whip closing on the outside. By the sixteenth pole, Shy Guy's lead was a head, but that was as close as Free America could get. McCreary didn't touch Shy Guy, who, as was his custom, was giving all he had. It was enough. Refusing to give an inch, he won by a head in a dead game performance.

When Free America returned to be unsaddled, Arcaro jumped off and said, "That's the dogginest little son of a bitch I have ever seen!"

Shy Guy was out of the High Time mare Tootsiecake. Tootsie had a sweet temperament, floppy ears and, like 57 percent of her sire's foals, had won as a two-year-old. Tootsiecake's first six foals all hit the ground running, and two of them won stakes, Shy Guy and Superwolf, a colt by Sweep All that won fourteen times, with two stakes wins in Chicago. Her seventh foal was a Spy Song filly, Kuchen, that didn't make it to the races but produced the good stakes winner Irongate and was granddam of three other stakes winners: Step Forward, Megaturn and Red Cross. Tootsie's eighth foal was Blitz Kuchen, by Spy Song. She won at two and was the granddam of the high-class stakes winner Fast Hilarious, plus stakes winners Really Cookin and Cooky Green and steeplechaser Cooky. Tootsie's last foal was Dresden Doll, a filly by Spy Song that broke her shoulder at Washington Park in the summer of 1956. I had the unhappy task of holding the shank while she was euthanized.

At one point in Shy Guy's career, he was sent back to the farm to be freshened, and it fell upon me to hot walk and graze him. Now that was a task! Especially grazing him. On more than one occasion, he had me up and down the shank like a yo-yo, but I managed to hang on. I was afraid to turn him loose. Dad would've killed me.

COLONEL DICK

One of the great regrets in my life is that I never knew my maternal grandfather, Colonel Richard Menefee Redd. He passed away shortly after my birth at age ninety-two. He was well known in Central Kentucky and beyond and was called Colonel Dick by everyone. My grandfather was never a colonel, but he looked like one. He was quite a horseman and a Confederate veteran. He was sixteen when he ran away from home to join his two older brothers, who were with General Jo Shelby in Missouri. It was there that he contracted yellow fever and nearly died, so I'm lucky to be here.

Colonel Dick. *Author's collection.*

Anyway, he brought home his uniform, sword, pistols and spurs and would lead parades in Lexington. Gave a great Rebel yell. My mother loved to tell the story of standing on Main Street in Lexington watching a Labor Day Parade when a lady behind her remarked, "Look at ol' Colonel Dick, leading the Labor Day Parade and never worked a day in his life."

Colonel Dick went everywhere on horseback. I doubt that he even knew how to drive a car. He once rode his horse Major up the courthouse steps in what was described in the newspaper as "a remarkable display of horsemanship," and, I was told, into the lobby of the Phoenix Hotel. And he was a teetotaler, lay preacher and onetime county assayer. He was still riding up until a few weeks of his death. He was preaching at the Belmont Chapel, which was on August Belmont's Nursery Stud, and that's where my father met my mother. Dad was employed by Belmont at about the same time, and Mom and Dad were married after he came back from the service. Mom's maiden name was Ruth Menefee Redd, and yes, I spelled Menefee correctly. Menifee County was named after one of my ancestors, Richard Menefee, but it was misspelled. He was a U.S. senator from Lexington, but he died shortly after the election.

I have copies of a postcard that was readily available during Colonel Dick's lifetime. You could mail a postcard for one cent at the time. On the stamp side, it reads, "Richard Menefee Redd, commander of the John C. Breckenridge Camp, C.S.A., and the chaplain of a community church where members of nine different denominations worship God under the same vine and fig tree, Jews, Catholics, Episcopalians, Methodists, Presbyterians, Lutherans, Baptists, Nazarenes, Christians. Our creed is God is Love. As God said, 'a new commandment I give you, love one another.'" On the flip side, in color, is a battle scene with my grandfather in full Confederate uniform, sword and all, mounted, with the quotation, "Stand still, Major my steed, and view the scene of carnage."

Major was the first horse I can remember seeing as a child. He came to live with us when we lived on Iron Works Pike after Colonel Dick passed away.

LEXINGTON

Lexington of today is nothing like the Lexington of my youth. The completion of the interstate highways, I-64 and I-75, in the late 1950s and early 1960s, completely changed the city. Up until that time, Lexington's population was about forty-five thousand, and it had a small-town atmosphere. I hate the traffic now and give thanks every day that I live in Bourbon County.

I can recall when you couldn't walk a half a block on Main Street without seeing several people you knew. Now it's who the heck are all these people and where did they come from, and of course, Main Street is nothing like it used to be. Christmastime in Lexington was fun. Big crowds. At least three five-and-dime stores, big department stores and six movie theaters. I remember the big display of model trains in Purcell's Department Store, seven or eight trains running in every direction imaginable. Mom would have to drag me away. With an allowance of fifty cents, you could go to a movie—double feature of course—then get a chicken salad sandwich and a root beer at one of the local drugstores. There was a big Sears Roebuck and a Montgomery Ward department store, too.

Lexington even had its own dog, Smiley Pete, so named because of his amiable expression. The local newspapers—there were two at the time—used to run notices asking people to not feed Smiley Pete because he was getting too fat. He lived downtown on the corner of Main and Limestone in a restaurant. It was a sad day when Smiley Pete passed away. He was buried with a marker bearing his name and date of death—no one had the vaguest idea of his date of birth. He was buried on North Broadway on property then occupied by the *Thoroughbred Record*, a weekly magazine devoted to horse racing and breeding.

By the time I was a teenager, I knew the locations of at least seven bookies. There were likely more, but the seven I knew about had the wire service. The biggest, at least the biggest I was ever in, was the one most frequented by Dad. It was in the Drake Hotel on Short Street just a half block off Broadway. The lobby had a large portrait of my grandfather Colonel Richard Redd. I have often wondered whatever happened to that portrait when they tore down the Drake. It's a parking lot now. The other entrance was to the bar. You had to walk through the bar, open a door that led to an alley, then go through another door that was the entrance to the bookie. Immediately on your right was a cage-like structure with a guy wearing, I swear, a green eyeshade. This is where you placed your bets and took your slips to collect your winnings.

It was a big room. All down one side was a platform with a guy with headphones listening to the wire service. Entries with odds, scratches, track conditions and any other pertinent information were chalked in on a large blackboard. The guy would announce the races as the information came over the wire from the tracks in action giving off the times, the 1, 2, 3 runners at the quarter, half, stretch and finish and chalk in the payoffs with the numbers when they became available. *Daily Racing Forms* were provided, or you could buy one for a quarter. Desks were scattered about so you could sit down to handicap. It was fun to go in with Dad and say hello to the mayor or the chief of police and other supporters of the industry.

There was another bookie located just three blocks down from the Drake at Keith's Bar. I liked that one because Dad would give me change to play the pinball machine. Then there was another one right next to the State Theater, at the Mayflower Bar. The State Theater was virtually next door to the Kentucky Theater, the only theater that survives today. The Ben Ali, Strand and Ada Meade are gone. The Opera House on Broadway no longer shows films but has been developed into a cultural center. When I was a kid, most of the films at the Opera House were Westerns, and there was always a short film featuring such stars as the Lone Ranger. Loved to sit in the balcony and watch the Lone Ranger. There was a Piggly Wiggly grocery store on the corner of Short and Broadway next door to the Opera House, and right across the street was where Frank Pieratt opened the first Applianceland when he got out of the service after World War II. Frank was a nice guy, and Pieratt's Applianceland thrives today under the management of his son, Bruce. His granddaughter, Nicole, owns Sallee Horse Van Service. Wonderful family.

The two most popular hotels downtown were the Lafayette and the Phoenix. The Lafayette still stands, but it is not used as a hotel anymore. The Phoenix is gone. For years, both were gathering places for horsemen. When John E. Madden purchased the land on Winchester Road that became Hamburg Place, he made sure that it was an easy buggy ride from the Phoenix so he could take customers to the farm. The Thoroughbred Club of America used to be located in the Phoenix, and right across the street, next to the Ben Ali Theater, was an upscale restaurant named the Golden Horseshoe. There was a large mural in the Golden Horseshoe that had the likenesses of many prominent horsemen of the time. Dad was in the mural. The Canary Cottage, next door to the Lafayette, was a popular place to eat. This was before the arrival of the fast-food joints.

I guess I was about ten when I was given permission to hitchhike to town on Saturday mornings to go to the movies. There were usually two, sometimes three of us, including Jimmy Hutchins, who lived just a field away from me on Dixiana, and Lucian Terrell, whose family operated the Jot 'Em Down Store on the Russell Cave Pike. It was no problem getting a ride. Many years later, while in the service, I hitchhiked home from California twice. It was no problem then, either. Just wear your uniform with the service ribbons, and it helped if you limped a bit. I had a friend in the service who had broken a foot in a basketball game and was on crutches. Everybody liked to go on the town with him, because when you walked into a bar, drinks were usually on the house. I certainly do not recommend hitchhiking today!

ERIN TORCH

I saw my first horse race in the fall of 1939 at Keeneland. I went with Mom and Dad to see a horse named Erin Torch run. I was eight at the time but can remember the race like it was yesterday. The distance was at a mile and a sixteenth, which meant that they broke right in front of the grandstand. It was on dirt, of course, there was no turf track at the time. Erin Torch broke in front and, as the saying goes, improved his position to win by eight. Four days later he was in again. Same distance, same result. I was hooked for life.

Erin Torch was bred by Mr. Fisher and was a foal of 1933 by Torchilla out of Irish Poly, by Polymelian. He won the Ontario Stakes as a four-year-old but had slipped down in class when I saw him run. His first win that I saw was for claiming tag of $1,050, the second win for $1,450. I know that sounds dirt cheap, but the year was 1937, so you can multiply that by about fifty to compare with today's purses. He was a gelding, and somewhere down the line, he was claimed from Dixiana.

In 1945, he was entered in a claiming race at Detroit, a race for lower-class claimers. Erin Torch had won forty-four races and was twelve years old, but he gave it his best. He got beat by a neck. Mr. Fisher claimed him, and he came home to Dixiana.

Erin Torch was a big horse, close to 17 hands, bay with black mane and tail and a small star. Dad made his rounds on the farm on Erin Torch, and during the summer, I would ride with him. The farm had installed a telephone in the big saddle horse barn and it would ring loud enough for the guys working in the barn to hear it and answer the call. We were there one day, and Dad was talking to one of the grooms when the phone rang and Erin Torch did what he had done 165 times at the races. He broke running. There was no starting gate, of course, but he knew what he was supposed to do when the bell rang. It caught Dad by surprise, but he stayed on—although it took him a good sixteenth of a mile to pull Erin Torch up. I learned a few new words that day.

A couple of years ago, I was watching TVG, the racing channel, when one of the so-called experts made the remark that the lower-class claiming horses are cheap because they have no heart. Well, I'd like to introduce him to Erin Torch, who had run 165 times, won 44 races and was still giving his best at age twelve. I've been muting that guy ever since!

Erin Torch was the first foal produced by Irish Polly. She was the dam of eleven winners from twelve foals, and her lone non-winner was a stakes producer. Erin Torch, in addition to winning the Ontario Stakes, placed in seven other stakes, including the Washington Park Juvenile as a two-year-old. He was a half brother to Irish Sun, a colt by Sun Again, that won the Lafayette Stakes and set a new track record at Keeneland over the about-four-furlong Headley Course. Another half brother, Irish Brush, by Dark Jungle, ran third in Keeneland's Breeders' Futurity in 1954 to Brother Tex, a colt owned and trained by Woody Stevens with Traffic Judge second.

Once again, somebody knew what they were doing when Mr. Fisher bought Irish Polly. She won as a two-year-old and again at three, but hers was not much of a pedigree. A full brother had placed in the Fordham Claiming Stakes, a race that doesn't ring many bells, and you have to go to the third dam to find a stakes winner. But there's no getting away from the fact that Irish Polly did herself proud as a producer.

At the time that Erin Torch returned home there was an annual event at the Red Mile, the local trotting horse track, called the Plug Horse Derby. The races were, as I recall, at a quarter mile and entries came from the horse farms around central Kentucky. They even had a mule race to go with the plugs. There was no parimutuel betting, of course, but a lot of money changed hands and a good time was had by all. There were usually five or six races on the card. Well, there was some talk at Dixiana of entering Erin Torch. The question was how could they hide the fact that the old boy was a Thoroughbred just off the tracks. Don't know if the powers that be, better known as the officials, at the Plug Horse Derby got wind of the plot or that the guys at Dixiana just gave up the idea of trying to make a sow's ear out of a silk purse, but Erin Torch never made it to the Plug Horse Derby. That would've been something to see!

Good Friends

DUVAL HEADLEY

Tom Fool was bred by Duval Headley, who owned Manchester Farm on Rice Road behind Keeneland. He also trained Menow for his uncle Hal Price Headley. Anyway, he sold Tom Fool privately to Greentree for either $20,000 or $25,000, depending on which account you read. Tom Fool had suffered a minor injury just prior to the sale, and some said the price was reduced.

Duval was another one of those people who was fun to be around. He bred a colt by an obscure sire that won stakes a few decades ago at Oaklawn. The dam of the colt had a nice pedigree; the sire was not well known. Looking back, I can't remember the sire's name. A few days later, I crossed paths with Duval at the Thoroughbred Club of America, and I asked him, "Why did you breed that mare to so and so?" "Aw, Ercel," he replied, "I burned the midnight oil planning that mating." Turned out, he had purchased the mare carrying that particular colt. You could never tell whether Duval was putting you on or not. One thing was for sure though. Duval had bought a future stakes producer. Sharp horseman. Runs in the family.

Duval also had stallions at Manchester Farm, and the one I remember best was The Axe II. The Axe II was bred by Greentree Stud. Duval syndicated him for stud duties and he did very well. "Everybody made money on that horse," I recall him saying. The Axe II was by Mahmoud, in fact, he was the most successful son of Mahmoud at stud, although Cohoes, another Greentree bred, did quite well. The Axe II excelled around two turns, winning such stakes as the Man o' War, the San Luis Ray and the Knickerbocker, and he sired thirty-nine stakes winners. The good sire Al Hattab was by The Axe II. He was bred by Arch Graham, who got his start with show horses and was a good friend of mine. Arch had leased a farm out on the old Richmond Road, and when he retired, he contacted me to see if I would be interested in picking up the lease. I was, and did, and for a number of years Henry White would send me a dozen or so weanling colts to board until they were ready to go to the sales or to be broken. Henry ran Plum Lane Farm, the old Hinata Farm, where Man o' War first entered stud.

Getting back to The Axe II, he also sired, among his thirty-nine stakes winners, Hatchet Man, a Greentree bred that won several major stakes. Hatchet Man was a pretty good sire, and his Executioner won the Flamingo, Metropolitan and Gulfstream Park Handicap. The most successful son at stud was Al Hattab, by The Axe II, bred by Arch Graham.

JIMMY DRYMON AND HERE DE ONE

Al Hattab, after winning sixteen races, seven of them stakes, was syndicated for stud duties by James D. Drymon. Jimmy had purchased a portion of the old Dixiana Farm and named it Domino Stud. He also syndicated the popular and successful Grey Dawn II, the excellent sire Dewan and the successful but not popular Nodouble. Nodouble was not accepted by Kentucky breeders because he was sired by Noholme II, who stood in Arkansas. After moving to Florida, Nodouble topped the sire list in 1981.

Jimmy Drymon was a great guy. He did a lot of nice, thoughtful things for people that nobody ever heard about. Jackie and I thought the world of him, in fact, we were business partners with him in a small way and even trained several horses for him. One was an older horse named Here De One that had been tried on the West Coast but had never won. He was by Dewan out of a mare by Round Table named Silver Settings. Silver Settings was a very well-bred mare that had been barren for several years for various reasons, and in fact, her only foal at that time was Here De One.

Jimmy owned a getaway on a small island in the Bahamas. Our vet at the time was Rachel Pemstein, and she was a good one. Rachel passed away much too soon. We had been teasing and checking Silver Setting on a regular basis, and Rachel told us that this mare needed to be bred now. This was in early February in about 1984. The breeding shed normally opened on February 15. So, we called Jimmy, who was at his getaway island home and told him that the mare needed to be covered. "Hell, Ercel the shed is not even open," was his reply. "Well open it." was my reply, so he called the farm and we took the mare over. I guarantee there was not a person in that breeding shed, including Jackie and me, who thought she could get in foal. But she did. Jimmy sold the result, a roan colt, for $18,000, and he won races. That was the last foal out of Silver Setting, but she was two for two as a producer, because we won several races with Here De One.

Let me tell you about Here De One. The first time we breezed him you could almost hear him change leads. He was pretty sore. It has been my experience that when someone tells you a horse is sour, it usually means he is sore. After curing that, we found another fault. He was slow. We trained him to go long, got him eligible for $5,000 starters, and he was never worse than third going a mile and an eighth or longer. He never tired. He was a local favorite at Turfway. We had a barrel of fun with that old horse.

Jimmy was a veteran of World War II. He flew a P-38 in the Pacific, and we were told he was the youngest fighter pilot ever to see action. Count your blessings when you have a friend like Jimmy Drymon.

Another tale of Here De One: We broke his maiden in a maiden special at Turfway. A few days later, I got a call from the stewards. They told me that he had tested positive for nicotine. Nicotine! I didn't know he smoked. Turned out, he had eaten a wad of tobacco that someone had spit out in the stall in the receiving barn at Turfway. Well, I didn't get another call from the stewards for over two weeks, so I entered him in a race for non-winners of two. Finally, I got a call asking me to check in with them when I brought the horse down to run.

I was running an entry that day, so I asked a good buddy of mine, Herb Jones, if he would saddle one of them for me, and he agreed to do so. The stewards' stand is located at the top of the grandstand at Turfway, and you had to get there by elevator. So, I went up and had a little chat with them. A couple of them were sitting there smoking, and that didn't set well with me and I told them so. Nicotine! No decision was made by the stewards. I left and took the elevator down. Herb was African American, and he was waiting to find out what happened. Herb knew that I was pretty disgusted with the whole situation, so I thought I would have a little fun with him. "Herb, I told them that you told me that they were all a bunch of no good sons of bitches!" I thought Herb was going to pass out. We had a good laugh over that.

Finally, the decision came down that there was no ruling against me, but they took the purse away. I guess everybody at Turfway knew what was going on. Here De One won that non-winners of two that night, and the track photographer, with a big smile, called him the "hero horse."

I must confess that I had one other ruling against me, and that was with the folks at River Downs. I had entered a horse in a grass race and it had rained and the stewards took the race off the turf and put it on the dirt. I called to scratch. The conversation went something like this:

"I want to scratch out of the third."
  "Why?"
"Because I want to run on the grass."
  "You can't do that."
"Why not? You can in Kentucky."
  "This is Ohio. If you want to scratch you have to vet him out."
"This horse is sounder than me. You want me to pay a vet to lie so I can lie to you?"
  "If you want to scratch call a vet."
"Every time somebody takes a leak at the eighth pole you take it off the grass."
  "That will cost you $50."
"Fine. It will cost me more than that to drive up there and run in a race that I don't want to be in."

So, after these many years, the only black marks against me are for a horse that chewed tobacco and for not lying to the stewards.

11

The Blood-Horse *and the* Daily Racing Form

In the spring of 1959, if memory serves, I left Dixiana to go to work with the *Blood-Horse*, a weekly magazine devoted to the turf that remains to this day my favorite. Get the *Blood-Horse* and the *Daily Racing Form*, and you are pretty much up on things. I spent the winter with four horses at Keeneland getting them ready for the Dixiana head trainer, Jack Hodgins, to pick up in the spring. I enjoyed that and was pleased that Dad had entrusted me with them. I also got a kick out of breaking yearlings, which I had been doing for several years.

Got to meet some really nice people at the *Blood-Horse*. Joe Estes was the editor. Very quiet, unassuming guy and a brilliant writer. He was to leave a few years later to gain access to the computers that were available at the Jockey Club. It was there that he devised the Average Earnings Index, which many still use today when considering matings. If you receive the *Blood-Horse*, you no doubt also get the Blood-Horse Stallion Register, and the Average Earning Index is available for every stallion with foals of racing age. The first time I crossed paths with Joe was at the funeral of Man o' War. He wrote the eulogy given by Ira Drymon and also gave a brief talk himself.

The advertising manager, Bill Worth, was my boss. I learned a lot from Bill. He taught me the yeas and nays of advertising, something I knew absolutely nothing about. Well, for good or bad, I've been writing advertising in one form or another for about sixty years. My favorite coworker at the *Blood-Horse* was Frances Kane. Frances was the daughter of Edward Kane, who had been manager of August Belmont's Nursery

Stud on the Georgetown Pike north of Lexington. He had passed away, and his wife had been promoted to manager at the time of Man o' War's birth. I have a great picture of Man o' War's sire, Fair Play, with Frances' brother Al holding him. Another favorite was Ruthie Hagyard, sister to famed veterinarian Dr. Charlie Hagyard. Two lovely ladies, and I do mean ladies. Frances and Ruthie worked in research.

Also in the research department was Art Baumhol, a native of New York. Art also had a radio show he called *Post Time* on a local station, giving the national race results six days a week every evening at 6:15.

There was no racing on Sunday in those days. It was a popular show because it was the first place a horseman could get results. The sponsors at the time were Keeneland and the Stallion Station, the latter owned by Lou Doherty. The Stallion Station may have been, but I won't bet the farm on this, the first farm to specialize in standing stallions. Art and I became friends, and he asked if I would fill in for him on occasions. That was my first venture into radio. Eventually, I was doing the show more than Art, and finally, he backed out. I kept on, and *Post Time* lasted for some fifty years, until computers and the internet made the show obsolete. I did the last *Post Time* show in August 2009, but by that time I was also doing another show about racing and breeding, *Horse Tales*, every Saturday morning. It's still on today from 8:00 to 10:00 a.m. on 105.5 FM in Lexington.

Getting back to my time at the *Blood-Horse*, which I enjoyed and learned a lot, Art and I decided to open our own advertising agency. We left the *Blood-Horse* in 1962 and opened Colin Advertising, and we were quite successful, but on December 1, 1967, I informed Art I wanted out. I didn't have the faintest idea what I was going to do, but out of the blue I got a call from advertising manager Leo Waldman of the *Daily Racing Form*. They wanted someone to specialize in advertising at the Kentucky Bureau of the *Form* which was based at Keeneland. I decided I would give it a shot and went to work for them on January 1, 1968. That was the same day that Ted Bassett came on as assistant to the president of the Keeneland Association, Louis Lee Haggin III. I hadn't been with the *Form* three weeks before I got in trouble. Mr. Haggin came into our office, looked around and said, "Ercel, you need more light in here." I told him I could see okay, which was true, but evidently, he went to Ted and complained about the lighting in the *Form* offices and I got a call from Ted. "Ercel, I don't appreciate your going over my head with a complaint." I had to talk my way out of that one. Ted is one of my heroes. A member of the greatest generation, ex-Marine and a great leader.

Mickey McGuire was the head of the Kentucky Bureau when I came aboard. There were just the two of us. Mickey covered the news and wrote a column that ran twice a week. I handled the advertising and wrote a column that appeared once a week. Mickey was an old-timer, a longtime employee of the *Racing Form*. He was in his early seventies, tall and trim, with silver-white hair and a recovering alcoholic. He had been sober for some forty years when I met him. He spent many years at the tracks making charts of the races. Mickey told me that he had spent one summer making charts at Dade Park, now Ellis Park, and couldn't recall a day. Said that friends had put him in a facility to dry out on occasion but that didn't work. All the attendants were bootlegging. Finally, he was in a hospital in Maryland; it was a terrible evening, deep snow, and a guy from Alcoholics Anonymous drove some forty miles to see him. "I didn't even know the guy," said Mickey, "and I figured anybody that would go to that much trouble to help somebody he didn't even know must be on to something. That was over forty years ago, and I haven't had a drink since."

Mickey was from Canada and loved ice hockey. He could never get over the fact that nearly everybody in Kentucky's favorite sport was basketball. "They score so many points that it's boring." Preston Madden named a horse Mickey McGuire. He was sired by Madden's home stallion, T.V. Lark, who topped the sire list in 1974 while standing at Hamburg Place. Mickey McGuire could run, and when he started winning, I would tease Mickey, "If he wins one more race then he'd have more class than you." He won a couple of stakes on the West Coast and was pretty good at stud, siring twenty-one stakes winners.

Mickey retired, as I recall, about 1972, and I was appointed director of the *Form*'s Kentucky Bureau. He had lost his wife to cancer several years earlier and had remarried, was doing a lot of traveling and having fun. I had built up the advertising by this time and needed help, especially with the columns and news coverage. That was not my field of expertise. I hired a great guy who turned into a dear friend, Logan Bailey, from the *Thoroughbred Record*. One day, I got a call from Mickey. "Could you and Logan stop by the house and see me for a few minutes?" I said of course. So, Logan and I drove to his house in Lexington and sat down, wondering what he wanted. It turned out that he had cancer. He had watched his first wife die a slow and painful death fighting the disease, and he was not going to do that. "Would you boys be pallbearers at my funeral?" That was a painful moment, tough to handle, as we were both fond of Mickey. He passed on a few months later.

One of the first of many people who I got to know while I was with the *Racing Form* was Fred Ross. Fred was in his nineties, couldn't have been much over five feet one or two and walked with a cane. He had spent a lifetime on the tracks as a trainer and a former steeplechase rider. He even dealt cards in a casino in Cuba. He lived in Lexington, out off East Main Street, when I first met him and owned a 1949 Ford that he would drive out to see us and to read the *Form*. The *Daily Racing Form*'s offices were in the Keeneland clubhouse in a section that had once been stalls. Keeneland charged stall rent for the three former stalls that we used.

Fred spent a lot of years training on the West Coast, but he had been all over working with horses in one capacity or another. He talked of being at a steeplechase meeting in Georgia. "Things were really hard. We were just one jump away from starving. They used to have a lot of chicken fights down there, and we would go to the fights and pick up the losers." He talked about being seriously injured in a fall when a horse went down with him. "A doctor gave me just months to live. I've been pissin' on that doctor's grave for forty years."

Fred eventually had to sell his car and move out of his apartment. He rented a small room at the YMCA, the one on High Street directly across from where the *Blood-Horse* was located at the time. He kept a small hotplate in his room and would cook his meals. He wasn't supposed to, but I think the management knew and overlooked it. Since he was no longer driving, I would drop copies of the *Form* off for him to read. When Fred passed away, I got a call from a lawyer he had contacted. I was to go to the bank and look in the safety box he had rented and, if there was any cash, give it to the Salvation Army. I did and there was $3,000 in $100 bills. The folks at the Salvation Army were impressed. I was also given instructions to scatter his ashes at Keeneland. I never did ask for permission from the powers that be at Keeneland. I was afraid they would say no, so I waited until almost everybody had gone home for the day then went out to the eighth pole and got the job done.

I stayed with the *Daily Racing Form* for some fifteen years. They were great to work for; get the job done, and they left you strictly alone. But I wanted to spend more time training a few of my own horses and resigned.

THE TEASER

I bought my first broodmare back in the 1960s. Dad had leased a small farm, I guess about fifteen acres, east of Lexington for a place to keep Larrikin, who had retired from racing. When Dad passed away in 1964 I took over the lease, and since I had to take care of Larrikin every day, I thought I might as well have a broodmare or two. That meant that I needed a teaser. That's how the horse business gets you hooked. Start taking care of one old gelding and you wind up with a barn full of horses.

Teasers come in all shapes and sizes, and they are used to see if the mare is receptive to the male for breeding. If the mare is in heat, she will let you know. You lead the teaser to the mare, and he checks her out as stallions do; if the mare is ready, she'll let you know by standing quietly. If they are not in the mood, they also let you know by kicking and squealing. I remember taking a mare over to Midway to be bred to a stallion named I Will that was standing at Hurstland Farm, owned by the brothers Charles, Alfred and Hiram Nuckols. She was a young maiden mare that had responded positively to the teaser, but when they led in I Will, she raised all kind of hell. They had two shanks on her with a man on each side of her head. Charles Nuckols was on one side and he looked over to the other guy and said, "Don't you let me out pull you." We didn't get her bred that day, but I took her home and let the teaser jump her, without penetration of course, until she got the idea. Took her back to Hurstland the next day and we got her in foal.

My first teaser was Buck, a medium-sized buckskin, that Dad had used at Dixiana. Buck had been retired from teasing at Dixiana. The spirit was willing but the flesh was weak. A lot of us old folks can relate to that. He worked out for a couple years but one day Buck got down and couldn't get back up. Had to send him to that great broodmare band in the sky.

So, I needed another teaser, called around and leased one for the breeding season for $350 payable in advance. Named him Ace. He was on the small side but big enough. He had big ideas. At the end of the season I called the guy and told him to come pick Ace up. He never showed. At the beginning of the next breeding season, he called and said he was coming to pick up the $350 for the upcoming season. I said fine, and I have a bill for you for eight months' board. Never heard from him again, and Ace stayed with me for the next twenty years or so.

Sometime during Ace's stay with us a couple of friends of Jackie's, old high school buddies, dropped by the farm for a visit. They knew nothing about horses, especially teasers. Over the years, Ace had developed a prominent crest to his neck. Jackie explained what Ace's job was, and one of her friends, Del Claire, asked, "How often does he get to, you know, you know?" Jackie told her just a couple of times over the past fifteen or twenty years with a pony that belonged to a friend. Del's eyes got big, and she said, "Oh my God, it's backed up all the way in his neck!"

Down through the years Ace must've bitten me one hundred times. The little jerk. One evening I was walking past his paddock and he was at the gate and nickered to me. He had never done that before. He wanted attention. He didn't seem to be in any discomfort but we gave him Banamine anyway. The next morning we found him dead in his paddock. He had been trying to tell us something, maybe goodbye. I still miss him.

DUCK OUT THE DOOR

In 1976 I bought a little mare named Duck Out the Door at the November Sale at Keeneland for, as I recall, $5,500. She had already produced three winners and was in foal to a French stallion named Kamaraan II. Nobody ever heard of Kamaraan II, and I remember talking to John Finney about him and John telling me that, "if you have to explain it, you are in trouble." I knew that, but I wanted the mare because she had been a hard-hitting runner at the races. I sold the Kamaraan II colt as a two-year-old in training with another colt by Pago Pago in a package deal for $15,000. Veterinarian Bob Copelan came to inspect them for a buyer and turned them down. He was right, of course. Bob was seldom wrong, and neither colt turned out to be worth a ham sandwich. But I got them sold.

I bred Ducky to Our Michael, a son of Bolero that was standing at Henry White's Plum Lane Farm, and she produced a nice-looking filly that I named That's Just Ducky. She could run a bit, and we sold her in training as a two-year-old for $17,000. She later produced a colt named Hard Rock Crossing that won the Swinford Stakes at Woodbine. Our Michael, incidentally, was blind and he was later sent to California for stud duties. I have often wondered about that.

Anyway Ducky, as we called her, produced six straight winners for us and we sold the first five before they started. The sixth, a colt by Hard Work named Whoosh, we decided to keep, something we did not do very often. T.A. Grissom told me many years ago, "It was better to sell one and be sorry than keep one and be sorry." Good advice. But we kept him anyway and he won some nice races for us.

Getting back to Duck Out the Door, it was through her that I met Allen Jerkens. I was working for the *Daily Racing Form* at the time and our offices were in the Keeneland clubhouse. Anyway, Allen had shipped in for the spring race meet and he came walking into the office, introduced himself and asked if I owned a mare named Duck Out the Door—if I did, he would like to go see her. So, we hopped in the truck and drove to the farm. We were a good two hundred yards away from where she was turned out with several other mares but Allen spotted her right away, climbed the fence and walked out into the field to pet her. She was bred by Hobeau Farms and Allen had trained her, winning seven races with her—including an overnight handicap at Tropical Park called the Miss Miami Handicap. "She was dead game," Allen said. Ducky was by Carry Back, a horse I went out of my way to see when I was in Ocala for a sale, out of a mare named Gold Duck, by Beau Gar. Definitely Florida breeding.

A few years later, Allen stopped by the farm and bought a two-year-old filly I had in training at the time. She was by Pago Pago, champion two-year-old in Australia in 1960 that had been imported by A.B. "Bull" Hancock for stud duties at Claiborne Farm. I sold the filly to Allen for $18,000 and he named her All My Marys and won the Politely Stakes. She beat a well-bred filly by the Claiborne Farm stallion Nijinsky II that later sold for $1 million at Keeneland as a broodmare. It was about this time that Pago Pago was moved from Claiborne Farm to Florida for stud duties. I bumped into Seth Hancock at a July yearling sale at Keeneland and told him, "Hell, Seth, you sent the wrong horse to Florida." Seth just smiled. He doesn't ruffle easily. I had bred to Pago Pago because he could get you a runner and the price was right, $1,000 live foal. He sired fifty-five stakes winners during his career.

I forgot to mention that Duck Out the Door's second dam was the Spy Song mare Gold Duchess, winner of the Thelma Stakes at the Fair Grounds and a full sister to the hard-hitting Duc de Fer. Gold Duchess also was a half sister to Duc d'Or, a colt by Spy Song's unraced full brother, Mr. Music, that won the Bay Shore Stakes

Duc de Fer was a flat runner. He won twenty-three races, nine stakes, and among them the Interborough Handicap in New York, the Myrtlewood in Chicago, the San Carlos in California, the Laurel Sprint Stakes in Maryland and the Oceanport in New Jersey. He was obviously a good shipper. As memory serves, Duc de Fer, a foal of 1951, was bred by a friend of Miss Mary's, Warfield Rogers, from Tennessee. Jackie and I kept Ducky on our farm in Bourbon County until she told us she wanted to go. She was over thirty when she died. She left us with lots of good memories.

ROCKY

In 1982, Jackie and I bought a mare named Curley's Valentine out of the November Sales at Keeneland. We already had three mares that we were breeding and wanted a fourth. Our requirements included a good race record and decent conformation. Couldn't afford a mare with a good pedigree to go with it, and Curley filled the bill. She was in foal to a horse we had never heard of, Breezing On. The mare was sired by Torsion, a son of Never Bend that had been a flop at stud. She was a big, handsome mare with a slightly clubbed left front hoof, but she had won eight times competing in allowance races and high-class claimers. She, as you might imagine, was cheap. I think we paid about $5,000 for her.

Breezing On was in New York and someone had claimed five or six good race mares to breed to him and put them in the sale. He had won minor stakes, the Hirsch Jacobs, and was by the decent sire Stevward, a son of Nashua. Years later, out of curiosity, I checked out Breezing On's record as a sire. In six crops he had sired fifty-eight foals, fifty starters, forty-four winners and seven stakes winners. By my old Russell Cave School math, that meant 12 percent stakes winners from foals. Looked like all he needed was an opportunity.

We named Curley's foal, a colt with a crooked stripe shaped like a backward question mark, Fifty Ways, after a popular song of the day, "Fifty Ways to Leave Your Lover." It wasn't long before we were saying fifty ways to lose your money! We nicknamed him Rocky because as a foal he had this habit of rocking back and forth, kicking up behind while never taking the slack out of the shank. He had a great personality and was one of our favorites. Should've known better. T.A. Grissom told me many moons ago, "Never fall in love with horses or ladies of the night." Cleaned that up a little bit.

We took our time getting him to the races. We always sold the ones that showed something in training, but Rocky didn't. He never saw a horse he could outrun in the morning. One of the outriders at the time told me one day, "Ercel, some horses were not meant to be race horses." Well, we took our time, put in lots of miles and finally got him ready to run. We put him in at Turfway, last race that night, for $5,000 maiden claimers going six furlongs. Hauled him down in our trailer. He hadn't been in one in at least two years, and never at night. We led him over, put up a bug rider named Sam Battaglia (no relation to Mike) and crossed our fingers.

Fifty Ways winning his first start, much to the surprise of all, on October 1, 1987. *Pat Lang, track photographer, Turfway Park.*

Rocky had drawn the eight hole in a ten-horse field, and he broke okay. He moved along in the middle of the pack until he turned for home and was still about five lengths back at the sixteenth pole. Then the light must've gone on in Rocky's mind. He took off and came flying to win by a head. We couldn't believe it. What a fun ride home. We laughed all the way and couldn't wait to see that outrider.

There are good cheap horses and there are bad cheap horses. Rocky was good. Every time we needed a little cashflow, Rocky would get us a check. We finally lost him in a claiming race at River Downs, but we kept our eye on him. We had a friend there and asked him to watch Rocky and the minute he looked like he was through to call us. The call finally came, and Jackie called the owner, who told her that he might have one more race in him. Jackie said, "No he doesn't. We don't even want his papers and will give you $300 for him." The man said come get him. Rocky lived to be nineteen. Never been around a nicer horse. Our daughter, Betsy, would ride him and he took good care of her.

We got five foals out of Curley, and four won. Had some fun with a filly named She's Not Nice, by Going Straight. Took us a while to win with her, but then she won three in a row, paying win prices of $42.00, $25.80 and $32.60. That 20–1 win came right before Christmas. Very timely. We found her a home with a young lady from Texas who would send us pictures of her foals. She used her as a jumper. She had a nice home.

12

Training

ALICE SCOTT

During the years that Jackie and I operated a racing stable based at the Thoroughbred Training Center on the Paris Pike, we devoted 90 percent of our efforts to training homebreds. We figured that if we screwed up it would be with our own horses, not somebody else's. You keep your friends that way. One day out of the blue, we got a call from Alice Scott. Now, Alice was a hoot. Life was a party for Alice, and she was fun to be around. She and her husband, Dan, owned a farm on Russell Cave Pike north of Lexington. Cross the interstate today going north and the first farm on the right belonged to Dan's brother, Harrie, Shandon Farm. The second farm on the right was Dan and Alice's.

Now, Alice was hard to say no to, so when she said, "I want you to train a horse for me," I agreed without asking who or what about the horse. It turned out to be a five-year-old gelding named Great Fate. Alice called him "Babyface." After we had taken over for a few days, we added Nelson to that. He also came with a pair of quarter cracks. As the old saying goes, at least he was going even. He was as sore on his left front as he was on his right front. He was also cheap, a $5,000 claimer at his best.

So, I called Alice and told her it would cost a small fortune to get him back to the races. "I don't care, I just want to win one more race with him." I should've known better, but once again I couldn't say no to Alice even

Great Fate, the longest shot I ever saddled. He won at River Downs on July 27, 1992, paid $127.40, $40.60 and $14.80. Owner Alice Scott on my left. *Pat Lang, track photographer, River Downs.*

though the chances of making money with Nelson were slim and none. He also was a pain in the you know what. We hauled our horses to the races in our two-horse walk-through trailer, and the first time we ran him he pitched a wing ding and broke his halter before we had gone a half mile. We always carried an extra halter, so we fixed that problem, but I had to ride with him for the entire trip to River Downs. He ate hay the whole way, happy as a lark. The little jerk.

Finally, the day came when he was sound enough to run—but in bar shoes. No luck there. Eventually, his quarter cracks healed, and we were able to exchange the bar shoes for Queen's Plates. We entered him in a $3,500 claiming race for horses that had not won a race in forever. This was on July 29, 1992, at River Downs, and the track came up sloppy. The race was for a mile and a sixteenth; we had trained him to go long, and he came from next-to-last in the field of twelve to win by four. The track announcer called him the winner at the sixteenth pole, "you can put a circle around Great Fate," and he paid $127.40, $40.60 and $14.80. I still have the chart of the race.

Now all those reasons as to why he won that day sound logical, but I didn't have much confidence in him. Didn't bet a nickel. It was rumored later that Nelson wound up playing polo. I wouldn't bet on that either.

Alice must've been in her late seventies at the time, but I never had the nerve to ask. She was small and petite and drove a great big silver Cadillac. She had to peer under the steering wheel to see where she was going and she kept a wine cooler right next to her in the front seat. She would drive along, talking up a storm, pedal to the metal while sipping wine. I rode back from the races on one occasion with her, and she scared the dickens out of me! Alice was a delight.

Years ago, it was to Alice and Dan's farm that Alfred Vanderbilt sent Geisha from his Sagamore Farm in Maryland to Kentucky for the 1949 breeding season. She had been booked to Polynesian at Ira Drymon's Gallagher Farm, which was located directly across the Russell Cave Pike from the Scotts' farm. All they had to do was walk her across the road. Saved a van bill, but I assume Vanderbilt was not too concerned about that. The result of that mating was Native Dancer, Thoroughbred racing's first TV star. Native Dancer was gray and thus easily identifiable on the small black-and-white screens at the time.

Native Dancer won twenty-one of his twenty-two starts, losing only to Dark Star by a head in the Kentucky Derby. Years later, Vanderbilt went to inspect the newly erected statue of Secretariat at Belmont Park. After checking it out, he remarked, "I see they left room for the names of all those horses that beat him." He had a point. They would have added the names of Herbull, Master Achiever, Fleet 'n Royal, Angle Light, Sham, Onion and Prove Out, not to mention Stop the Music, who was moved to first on the disqualification of Secretariat in the Champagne Stakes.

Native Dancer just may hold the distinction of being the best racehorse not to be named Horse of the Year. He was a champion at two and a champion three-year-old, but Horse of the Year honors went in his sophomore year to Greentree's Tom Fool, a four-year-old that had won all ten of his starts in the handicap division. The two never met. Native Dancer's chief rival that year was Jamie K., a son of Crowfoot foaled on a farm located within the city limits of Paris, on Eighth Street in Bourbon County. He was life-and-death to beat Jamie K. in both the Preakness and the Belmont. Jamie K., incidentally, had a full sister, Nell K., that was also a talented runner. Native Dancer went on to immortality as the sire of Raise A Native and grandsire of Northern Dancer.

THOROUGHBRED TRAINING CENTER

Jackie and I trained for the better part of thirty years at the Thoroughbred Training Center just north of Lexington on the Paris Pike. The majority of those who train there reside in nearby counties, do all their training there and van to whatever tracks are open at the time. We had our own trailer, a two-horse walk-through, and ran at the Kentucky and Ohio tracks. Never did go to Mountaineer in West Virginia. We seldom trained for other owners, just trained our leftovers. By leftovers I mean homebreds that were either slow or wouldn't vet out—in other words, the ones we couldn't sell.

The Thoroughbred Training Center, or TTC, is a great place to train. The track is super safe and just deep enough for your horses to get a lot out of their workouts. There's a grass gallop and turnout paddocks, the barns are well-maintained and there is a facility with a swimming pool available. Great management. What more could you ask? The TTC is owned by Keeneland, which is another plus. We made a lot of friends and met a lot of nice people. It's a long list, but I'll single out a few. One of the first we met was Herb Jones, a guy I think the world of. Herb is four months younger than I am, but I tease him about being older. He's a terrific horseman. He's African American and came up when that was difficult to overcome, but he trained over five hundred winners down through the years. I know he trained many years ago for Buckland and also for Governor Brereton C. Jones.

I've had Herb on my radio show several times, and he always had great stories. How many were true is another matter. One time, I asked him how he got started on the racetrack:

> *The first guy I worked for was, I'm going to use a fictitious name here, was Joe Smith. He liked to gamble and I thought I could make an extra buck working there. One day he had a filly in and his mother stopped by the barn and asked if she had a good chance of winning a bet. He told her maybe next time but not today. That afternoon the filly won at better than 15 to 1. I knew right then that anybody that would stiff his own mother wouldn't give me a shot. I was on a plane the next day.*

I had a horse entered at Ellis Park one day and got a call from Herb. "Bring him to my barn and I'll have a stall ready for you." This was when he was training for Governor Jones, and he was having a terrific meet. His winning percentile was so high that the odds would drop on whatever he led over to run. To compound the situation, I had named the leading rider, Mike Moran, who was riding regularly for Herb, and the guy I hired to lead the horse over to run worked for Herb. Why my horse went off at 12–1 is a mystery, but it was likely because I was down as his trainer. We didn't run at Ellis Park very often. Well, Damnation was my horse's name, won by many and paid $25.40. After the race, there were those who accused Herb of running the horse in my name in order to win a bet. Herb did nothing to change their minds.

Damnation was fast but fragile. That was just his second start, and he came out of the race with an ankle problem. We turned him out and were able to win a couple more with him. Found him a home, and he became a big-time foxhunter in Virginia.

Herb was about as good at pointing a horse for a race as anyone I have ever seen. He was training at Detroit one year when word got out that the singing group the Supremes was going to make the trophy presentation in a race. Herb wanted to meet the Supremes, pointed a horse for the race and won it. Herb said, "I took them out to dinner, and by Monday morning, I had spent close to $3,000."

Another friend was Leonard "Grub" Atkinson. Herb, Grub and I were in the same barn together at the TTC. Carter Thornton also had a couple of stalls, as did Bob Faulk, a friend who passed away much too soon. Fun barn. Grub was from Michigan, and he left home at fourteen. Grub said, "My brother dropped me off at River Downs," and he has spent his life with horses. He had a mare, can't remember her name, but they called her Big Mary. He put a runout bit on her, stood her in ice before the race and ran her with bandages all around and would enter her on the bottom at River Downs. Nobody in their right mind would have claimed her and she won five in a row. Grub later sold her, and she became a stakes producer in South America.

Big Mary would kick you in a heartbeat. One day, I got to the barn a bit early and was alone, and Big Mary was cast against the wall in her stall. I went in the stall to get her up and managed to do so, and she wheeled and had dead aim on me. Scared the living daylights out of me. But for some reason, she didn't fire. I told Grub the next time she was on her own.

All in all, we had a great time training at the TTC. There's no greater thrill than winning a race with a homebred. I saddled my last horse in the fall of 2002 and spent the winter waking up at 4:30 in the morning, reading and working jigsaw puzzles. We still had a few horses, retirees, on the farm. There are four here as I write this that I'm trying to outlive.

They are the last two that I trained, a broken-down rescue and a mare that Jackie used to foxhunt. In the early winter of 2003, I got a call from Jim Pendergest, longtime manager of the TTC. In fact, he had survived several owner changes of the place and stayed on when Keeneland bought it in 2001 or 2002. Keeneland wanted a full-time clocker and Jim, knowing that I had quit training, asked if I would be interested. Well, I like Jim, he's a straight shooter and an accomplished manager, firm but fair. You always knew where you stood with Jim. So, I told them I would get them started. I stayed for ten years.

The only bone I have to pick with Jim is that he told me that I would have about 40 works per week to turn in. Wrong! Within a couple of weeks, I hollered for help. I needed someone to write down the names and the times while I did the clocking. Various people would come after the break to help. Every morning, there's a half-hour break to renovate the track surface then, when the track reopened, the roof would fall in. People would flood the track with workers. One day Jackie stopped by to help, and we recorded 117 works. Jim happened to be standing behind us, and when we could finally come up for air, he said, "That was ugly." So much for 40 works a week! But it was fun, and as with everything else you do with horses, you learn a lot. As a matter of fact, I couldn't believe they were paying me to watch horses. I would've done it for nothing but I never told them that.

I continued to do the clocking for ten years and would've stayed, except I was starting to lose my hearing. I always had difficulties understanding the Hispanics, but when it advanced to the stage that I was having trouble with the Irish, I knew it was time to hang up my watch. I gave Jim notice and blamed Jimmy Corrigan, one of the Irish trainers at the TTC and a friend of mine. I accused him of speaking Gaelic so I couldn't understand him. Actually, I'm a big fan of the Irish. Most have worked with horses all their lives, and they move the bar up when it comes to horsemanship.

Jackie and I bought this little piece of heaven where we live in Bourbon County in 1987. I was blessed with great parents, a lifetime spent with horses and horse people, children and grandchildren I am proud of, a wife that I adore and a great dog. Who could ask for more?

Bibliography

Estes, J.A. "Big Red." *Blood-Horse*, October 23, 1937.
———. "Reunion." *Blood-Horse*, May 16, 1931.
———. "Sweep All to Himself." *Blood-Horse*, May 30, 1931.
Hewitt, Abram S. "Double Jay," as told by A.B. Hancock Jr. in *Sire Lines*. Lexington, KY: *Blood-Horse*, 2006.
———. "High Time." In *Sire Lines*. Lexington, KY: *Blood-Horse*, 2006.
Runyon, Damon. Column in *Hearst* publications. May 17, 1930.

About the Author

Ercel Ellis Jr. has been a writer and editor for the *Blood-Horse* and the *Daily Racing Form*, plus broadcasting shows *Post Time* and *Horse Tales* for over sixty years and has recorded a CD of readings from Joe Palmer's *This Was Racing.* Born into the Thoroughbred horse business, he has been an owner, breeder, trainer, writer and broadcaster. He won the Kentucky Thoroughbred Owners and Breeder's prestigious Charles W. Engelhard Award for contributions to the Thoroughbred industry in Kentucky and is an honorary member of the Kentucky Thoroughbred Farm Managers Club. He lives on a small farm in Bourbon County, Kentucky, with his wife, Jackie, dog Spaniel Boone, four old retired Thoroughbred race horses and several barn cats.